Masterpieces of Wedgwood in the British Museum

MASTERPIECES OF
WEDGWOOD

IN THE BRITISH MUSEUM

Aileen Dawson

PUBLISHED FOR THE TRUSTEES OF THE BRITISH MUSEUM
BY BRITISH MUSEUM PUBLICATIONS LIMITED

© 1984 The Trustees of the British Museum

Published by British Museum Publications Ltd,
46 Bloomsbury Street, London WC1B 3QQ

British Library Cataloguing in Publication Data

Dawson, Aileen
　　Masterpieces of Wedgwood in the British Museum.
　　1. Wedgewood ware —— History
　　I. Title
　　738.2′3　　　NK4335

ISBN 0–7141–0531–7

Designed by Sebastian Carter

Set in Monophoto Plantin
and printed in Great Britain by
W. S. Cowell Ltd, Ipswich

**The Trustees of the British Museum wish to
acknowledge with special gratitude the generous
assistance that has been received towards the cost
of the colour plates of this book from Josiah
Wedgwood and Sons Ltd, through the interest in
the project expressed by Sir Arthur Bryan.**

Front cover Blue jasper ware copy of the Portland Vase.
The original is a cameo-glass vase of the 1st century AD in
the British Museum. Most of Josiah Wedgwood's copies
were made in black jasper (see Pl. 9). This vase may have
been made during the period of experimentation *c.* 1790
or not long after his death in 1795. H. $9\frac{3}{4}$ in (24.7 cm).
Presented to the British Museum by John Wedgwood,
1802.

Back cover Black basalt portrait medallion of Josiah
Wedgwood in gilt metal frame; incised W. H on shoulder
for William Hackwood, who modelled the portrait in
1782. H. (not incl. frame) $4\frac{1}{8}$ in (10.3 cm).

Frontispiece Blue and white jasper ware griffin candlestick
(one of a pair) after a design by Sir William Chambers,
published in 1792, impressed WEDGWOOD, late 18th
century (see Fig. 44, p. 57).

Contents

Preface

Josiah Wedgwood (1730–95) is very often considered as the most remarkable of all English potters. Living in a period of particularly rapid social and industrial change, he took full advantage of growing markets to build up an immensely successful business. The only potter ever to be made a Fellow of the Royal Society, his life embraced more than business and was marked by constant experimentation into ceramic technique and practice. Over a working life of three decades or more he perfected a range of new ceramic bodies, devised well over 100 vase forms which were often based on classical prototypes, produced plaques ornamented with reliefs for chimneypieces, suites of cameos and intaglios often based on classical engraved gems, carrying on a partnership with Thomas Bentley (1730–80) for the 'ornamental' wares, and with his cousin Thomas Wedgwood (1734–88) for domestic articles. The impetus continued into the early years of the nineteenth century when the firm was run by Josiah's nephew Thomas Byerley (c. 1747–1810) and his sons John (1766–1844) and Josiah Wedgwood II (1769–1843) in turn. Despite some difficulties in the 1840s, the company survived and then began in the High Victorian age to enjoy renewed inventiveness and prosperity. The twentieth century saw it respond once more to changes in taste, and notably to the Modern Movement experienced in Britain in the 1920s and 30s. The exceptional riches of the British Museum's collection have enabled the author, using its masterpieces as illustrations, to give a survey of the history of the firm.

This book is not a catalogue of the collection; specially selected pieces only have been mentioned, and these have been chosen on the grounds of their particular technical or aesthetic merit or historical interest. These masterpieces are illustrated and described within the context of the history of the firm. When they are known to have been based on already existing objects, such as classical vases or sculpture, engraved gems, medals, contemporary sculpture or even on prints or book illustrations, these sources are drawn to the reader's attention. A broadly chronological approach has been adopted. Documentary sources have been used wherever possible to illustrate the progress of the firm and to provide evidence for dating its productions. References to documents from the accumulation now on loan to Keele University, Staffordshire (the property of Josiah Wedgwood and Sons Ltd) are given in the text beside quotations; otherwise they can be found in the notes at the end of the book. A few pieces have been mentioned which are not illustrated. Museum accession numbers for these will be found in the notes to each chapter.

The collection in the British Museum is the oldest and one of the most extensive in the British Isles. The donation made by Josiah Wedgwood himself marks its foundation, and the scene on his famous Pegasus Vase presented in 1786, based on a Greek painted earthenware vase from Sir William Hamilton's collection purchased by the Museum in 1772, demonstrates the potter's close identification with objects in the Museum. The second piece of contemporary pottery, as opposed to porcelain, ever to enter the collections was another piece of blue jasper ware presented in 1802 by the potter's eldest son, John Wedgwood (1766–1844). It again has close links with the history of the Museum as it is a direct copy of the famous Alexandrian cameo-glass Portland (or Barberini) Vase, which was brought to England by Sir William Hamilton in spring 1783, briefly belonged to the Duchess of Portland, was loaned to the Museum by the Portland family in 1810 and finally acquired in 1945. After these magnificent gifts, the collection grew steadily during the nineteenth century as 'old Wedgwood' became fashionable. In 1853 Joseph Mayer of Liverpool gave twenty-four pieces, mainly portrait medallions, and in 1878 Major-General A. Meyrick presented two remarkable early basalt plaques. Further minor gifts came from Felix Joseph in 1888 and W. J. Stuart in 1880 and 1890.

By the end of the nineteenth century, after the accession of the magnificent gift of Sir A. W. Franks, employed at the Museum between 1851 and 1896, the collection contained 700 pieces. They were catalogued in 1903 by R. L. Hobson in the *Catalogue of English Pottery in the British Museum*. At this time the chief strength of the collection lay in its cameos and intaglios, most of which have a clear link with the classical world in their subject-matter, and in the remarkable group of portrait medallions consisting of over 100 items, some of great rarity. In 1909 two great benefactors, Mr and Mrs Isaac Falcke, who had collected Wedgwood for over fifty years, presented around 500 pieces. They were principally jasper wares, basalt and some unusual creamware, especially ornamental creamwares with coloured bodies or glazes. Many pieces still have exhibition labels or pencil notes recording where they were on view during the course of the last century. The most recent scholarly study of the collection by Hugh Tait in articles published in the *Proceedings of the Wedgwood Society* in 1961 and 1963 gives a complete descriptive hand-list of creamware and pearlware including the many pieces acquired in 1909 and later. The growth of the collection has continued at a more moderate rate this century, with the emphasis on documentary items, source material and more recently on pieces from the later period of the factory's activity.

Acknowledgements

The author owes a particular debt of gratitude to the members of staff of the Wedgwood Museum, Josiah Wedgwood and Sons Limited, Barlaston, Staffordshire, Miss Gaye Blake Roberts, Mrs Lynn Miller and Mrs Sharon Gater for their tireless and invaluable help, cheerfully given. Dr Ian Fraser, formerly Archivist at Keele University Library, Mrs Margaret Morris and Mrs Christine Fyfe have given unstintingly of their time in checking references. Miss Jane Clarey has compiled the index. The staff of public collections and institutions in Britain, the United States of America and the Soviet Union have been unfailingly obliging: Ms Ann Eatwell, who provided much information on the Portland Vase and assisted in compiling the Appendix, Mrs Jennifer Opie and Robin Hildyard, Victoria and Albert Museum, South Kensington; Mr Revel Oddy, Royal Scottish Museum, Edinburgh; Miss Emmeline Leary, City Museum and Art Gallery, Birmingham; Miss Pam Wood, Nottingham Castle Museum; the staff at Hanley Museum, Stoke-on-Trent, Mrs Pat Halfpenny, Mrs Kathy Niblett and Mr David Barker who have all been particularly helpful; Mrs Harry Buten and the staff of the Buten Museum of Ceramics, Merion, Pennsylvania, USA; Mrs Louisa Bartlett and Miss Deborah Binder, St Louis Art Museum, Missouri; Miss Jessie McNab and Mrs Clare Le Carbeiller, Metropolitan Museum of Art, New York City; Mrs Lynn Roberts, the Art Institute of Chicago; the Ministry of Culture of the USSR for permitting me to study at the State Hermitage Museum, Leningrad, and the Director of that institution and his staff, in particular Miss R. Soloweitchik, Mrs L. Lyachkova and Mrs L. Voronikhina, and the staff at Pavlovsk Palace and Kuskovo Ceramics Museum. Many private individuals have also assisted me including Mrs Maureen Batkin, Mr Richard Dennis, Mr and Mrs John Desfontaines, Mrs Brixie Jarvis, Miss Alison Kelly, Mr Michael Raeburn, Mr and Mrs F. D. Rickerby, and in the USA Mrs Elizabeth Chellis, Mr Sidney Goldfein, Mr and Mrs Herbert Jacobs, Mr Lawrence Pucci, Dr and Mrs Leonard Rakow, Mr Bernard Starr, Judge and Mrs Trabue, and Mr and Mrs David Zeitlin. Finally I should like to thank the staff of the British Library, members of the Departments of Egyptian Antiquities, Greek and Roman Antiquities and Prints and Drawings and my colleagues in the Department of Medieval and Later Antiquities in the British Museum for their support, particularly Mr Neil Stratford and Mr Hugh Tait. The staff of the British Museum Photographic Studio, including Mr Tony Milton ARPS, have also made outstanding contributions.

Introduction:
Wedgwood's early years

Josiah Wedgwood was born in 1730, the seventh son and last of twelve children of
Thomas Wedgwood and his wife Mary Stringer. The date of his birth is not
known, but he was baptised on 12 July at St John's Church, Burslem, near
Newcastle under Lyme, Staffordshire. It is likely, therefore, that he was born
shortly before since, in an era when infant mortality was high, baptisms took place
not long after birth. His father was a potter at the Churchyard Works, whilst his
distant cousins John and Thomas Wedgwood were prosperous makers of salt-
glazed stonewares and lived in a rather splendid brick-built house known as the
'Big House'. Josiah attended school at Newcastle under Lyme, three and a half
miles from home, perhaps only until the age of nine when his father died. According to his teacher Thomas Blunt, the boy left school 'a fair arithmetician and
master of a capital hand'. In later life he was not in the least hampered by his lack
of education, and as a successful business man made sure that his children
received the best instruction available.

In 1739 Josiah was apprenticed to his eldest brother, Thomas, although formal
articles were not drawn up until 11 November 1744. The agreement specified that
he was to learn to handle clay and to throw pots on the wheel. It is probable,
though, that his usefulness was somewhat curtailed when he contracted smallpox
in 1742: after a long illness, which it is often said enabled him to cultivate a taste
for reading and thinking, he recovered to find that his right knee was affected so
that he was unable to operate the potter's wheel. Eventually the knee proved so
troublesome that the leg was amputated in May 1768. James Bent, a surgeon from
Newcastle under Lyme, performed the operation, which was referred to in a
postscript to an invoice of 28 May (L. 91-16514) sent by Peter Swift, Wedgwood's
'cashier, paymaster general and accountant' from 1766: '. . . . M.ʳ. Wedgwood has
this day had his leg taken of [sic] & is as well as can be expected after such an
execution . . .' Despite the terrible pain he must have suffered, he recovered
within a matter of weeks and thereafter used a wooden leg. Although he never
went abroad, the loss of the limb did not prevent him from travelling far from
home and from leading an extremely active life. After the end of his apprentice-
ship Josiah worked for his brother for three years, but was not taken into partnership, and left him in 1752 to join Harrison and Alders at Cliff Bank, Stoke. As
Alders had retired, Wedgwood worked with Harrison making salt-glazed and
lead-glazed wares. Mottled and tortoise-shell dishes are also said to have formed
part of their production.

The pottery industry was well-established in Staffordshire in the mid-
eighteenth century.[1] Because of its ample natural resources of low-firing red clays
and refractory white clays in close proximity to outcrops of coal, used from the
seventeenth century as fuel to fire the kilns, the area was fast becoming the leading
centre for pottery manufacture. In addition salt and lead supplies, which formed

the basis of glazes for stonewares and earthenwares respectively, were reasonably accessible in Cheshire and the Peak District. Clays from North Devon and Dorset for the production of white wares were being imported from about 1720 via a coastal route to Chester, then overland by pack animal or wagon to the Potteries.

Preparation of raw materials was still relatively primitive: clays were weathered outdoors for two or three years, then purified by levigation in water so that finer particles which came to the top could be drawn off and the water in them evaporated. In the 1730s, however, drying first began to take place indoors in a shallow kiln so that potters were less dependent on weather conditions. Ground flint from south-east England was used to achieve a whiter earthenware and to reduce the risk of warping in firing; but the grinding of flints was known to be harmful to health, and in an effort to combat the effects of dust Thomas Benson of Newcastle under Lyme took out two patents for the preparation of flints, the second using large stones in a wet grinding method. Both lead (powdered and in suspension in water) and salt were used for glazing, the latter for stonewares. Salt, which was thrown into the kiln when it was at bright-red heat ($1,200°$c), volatised, combining with the silica in the body to form a shiny glaze. It is important to remember that at this time every aspect of the industry was undergoing improvements.

The one hindrance to the expansion of the trade was the sorry state of the transport system. Ever-increasing amounts of pottery were being carried by packhorses, two crates at a time, or by wagon, frequently on roads with deep ruts which were filled with water in winter. (Such pot-holes are usually attributed to the potters' habit of digging their clay at the nearest convenient spot.) Water transport was confined to the River Weaver, made navigable as far as Winsford in 1733, the River Dee from Chester, the River Severn from Bridgnorth, and the River Trent from Willington to Hull. From the ports, particularly from Hull, the crates of ware were either sent around the coast to English destinations or exported direct. It was not unusual in the 1730s for potters to sell to dealers in London or even to own, or part-own, warehouses in London, and regular shipments of various types of Staffordshire pottery were sent to Europe by John Baddeley of Shelton before 1749,[2] disproving the claim made by some writers that Wedgwood was the first to open up European markets.

Within two years of its commencement in 1752 Josiah Wedgwood's association with Harrison and Alders gave way to a partnership with a much more famous and innovative potter, Thomas Whieldon of Fenton Hall. Whieldon, who was to outlive Wedgwood by two years, retired in 1780 with a fortune of £10,000. Josiah's conditions of employment included the right to make experiments for improving the wares, the details of which could remain secret. In his 'Experiment Book', still preserved at the Wedgwood Museum, is a preface giving an extremely clear idea of what he was doing during this period (E.26-19117):

> This suite of Experiments was begun at Fenton hall, in the parish of Stoke upon Trent, about the beginning of the year 1759, in my partnership with Mr Whieldon, for the improvement of our manufacture of earthen ware, which at that time stood in great need of it, the demand for our goods decreasing daily, and the trade universally complained of as being bad & in a declining condition.

> White stone ware (viz with salt glaze) was the principal article of our manufacture; but this had been made a long time, and the prices were now reduced so low that the potters could not afford to bestow much expence upon it, or make it so good in any respect as the ware would otherwise admit of. And with regard to Elegance of form, that was an object very little attended to.

> The article next in consequence to Stoneware was an imitation of Tortoiseshell. But as no improvement had been made in this branch for several years, the country was grown weary of it; and though the prices had been lowered from time to time, in order to increase the sale, the expedient did not answer, and something new was wanted, to give a little spirit to the business.

I had already made an imitation of Agate; which was esteemed beautiful & a considerable improvement; but people were surfeited with wares of these variegated colours. These considerations induced me to try for some more solid improvement, as well in the *Body* as the Glazes, the *Colours*, the *Forms*, of the articles of our manufacture.

I saw the field was spacious, and the soil so good, as to promise an ample recompence to any one who should labour diligently in its cultivation.

The 'Experiment Book' is a record of Wedgwood's trials which were conducted in a rigorously scientific manner at a time when established practice and rule-of-thumb methods were prevalent, although it is certainly true that the first half of the eighteenth century had seen considerable technical progress in the pottery trade. Wedgwood's record was coded so that the secrets remained his own. The green and yellow glazes for earthenwares seem to have put his business on a firm footing, so one can hardly blame him for his desire to keep the recipes to himself.

After five years with Whieldon, Wedgwood, aged twenty-nine, was ready to begin business on his own account. On 1 May 1759 he took out a lease on the Ivy House, Burslem, and its adjoining potworks, from his distant cousins Thomas and John Wedgwood, for a rent of £15 for the first year which included the use of two kilns, workshops and cottages. He was to remain here until about New Year 1764 and then seems to have moved to new premises at the Brick House, nearby at Burslem. He gave notice to leave his old premises in November 1769, although he did not complete the move until February 1773. His cousin, another Thomas Wedgwood, was taken on as a journeyman for six years from May 1759 (the memorandum of the agreement was signed on 30 December 1759) and, as it happened, was to remain associated with him until Thomas's death in 1788. In 1766, after finishing his service as Josiah's journeyman in the previous year, he became his partner for the manufacture of 'useful' or domestic wares with a one-eighth share of the profits of this part of the business. Later Josiah was to distinguish quite clearly between this domestic ware partnership and the partnership established in 1769 (see p. 25) with Thomas Bentley for the manufacture of ornamental pieces. These two aspects of Josiah's production will be treated in separate chapters.

1 The 'useful' partnership

The early years of Josiah's new enterprise with his cousin were spent in the manufacture of pieces similar to those he had made in association with Thomas Whieldon. One of the most popular types of pottery made in the mid-eighteenth century was known as red ware. Unglazed, it was made of local red clay usually prepared according to the recipe perfected at the end of the seventeenth century by the Dutch brothers, John Philip and David Elers. Wedgwood himself gave due credit to them, if his testimony, in a letter to Bentley of 19 July 1777 (E. 25-18772), can be taken at face value: 'The next improvement introduc'd by Mr. E. [John Philip] was the refining our common red clay, by sifting, & making it into Tea & Coffee ware in imitation of the Chinese Red Porcelaine, by casting it in plaister moulds, & turning it on the outside upon Lathes, & ornamenting it with the Tea branch in relief, in imitation of the Chinese manner of ornamenting this ware.'

The use of casting made possible the production of shapes which could not be thrown on the potter's wheel. In this method liquid clay, or 'slip', is poured into a plaster-of-Paris mould which absorbs the water content of the clay. The excess slip is poured off, and the clay dries and takes on the shape of the mould. When dry it can be easily removed because the clay shrinks. Many pieces, such as teapots, were made in several parts which were joined together with water before firing. Handles and finials were sometimes formed by hand or press-moulded and also attached to the piece using water. Decoration consisted of hand-modelled reliefs of vine trails in imitation of the Chinese, or alternatively of lathe-turned fluted and diced motifs.

Josiah Wedgwood is often credited by contemporaries with the earliest use of the rose engine-turning lathe for pottery decoration. He employed this method for creamwares as well as red wares, but examples of the latter that can safely be attributed to him are rare. Some pieces with imitation Chinese marks, which may include a w, may have come from his factory and are similar to fragments found at the Brick House site to which Josiah moved after his marriage in 1764. An engine-turned milk jug and cover in the British Museum collection bears this mysterious mark, as does a lid said to have been found on the Brick House site (Figs 1, 2a, 2b). It seems to have been presented to the Museum during the nineteenth century by Miss Eliza Meteyard who devoted much of her life to writing on Wedgwood, but there is no record as to when it entered the collection. Supplying red ware in large quantities enabled Wedgwood to establish himself, but he seems later to have developed a dislike for this material (see p. 45). However, in 1776 he gave it a new name, '*rosso antico*', and kept it in production for many years using it for ornamental pieces, often in combination with another body based on local clays, black basalt.

There was a strong demand in the middle of the eighteenth century for fine

Figure 1 (*top right*) Red ware
milk jug and cover, unglazed,
decorated with engine-turned
patterns; impressed imitation
seal marks including W on
base. A cover (*top left*) is said
to have been found on the
Brick House site, Burslem,
and presented, presumably to
the British Museum, by Miss
Eliza Meteyard; both *c.* 1764–9.
H. of jug and cover incl. knop
$4\frac{3}{4}$ in (12 cm). Diam. of lid $3\frac{1}{4}$ in
(8.2 cm). Jug and cover
bequeathed by A. W. Franks
Esq., 1897.

Figure 2a (*bottom left*)
Imitation Chinese marks
including W impressed on
underside of red ware cover of
jug (Fig. 1, *left*) said to have
been found on the Brick House
site, Burslem, and presented,
presumably to the British
Museum, by Miss Eliza
Meteyard.

Figure 2b (*bottom right*)
Imitation Chinese seal marks
including W impressed on base
of red ware jug (Fig. 1),
attributed to Josiah Wedgwood
at the Brick House site,
Burslem, 1764–9.

salt-glazed stonewares with moulded relief decoration often in the 'Chinese manner'. William Greatbatch, who was also apprenticed to Thomas Whieldon and later worked in Fenton (Staffordshire), is known to have been responsible for supplying Wedgwood with 'blocks' or master moulds made of wood or pitcher (fired clay). From these expendable working moulds in plaster of Paris were taken. A number of shapes (such as teapots and tea-caddies), as well as undecorated pieces of stoneware, were supplied by Greatbatch. Although he was the most gifted block maker of his time, Greatbatch sought Josiah's advice on shapes, as is evident in more than one surviving document. A number of his blocks were discovered early this century at the Wedgwood works, Etruria (Fig. 3), probably undisturbed since the eighteenth century. These provide valuable clues as to exactly what moulded pieces were made by Josiah, such as the cauliflower-moulded teapot from the British Museum collection shown in Fig. 4.

Recent excavations at the Greatbatch pottery site have brought to light many fragments which will assist in building up a picture of how the Staffordshire pottery industry functioned in the mid-eighteenth century. One moulded pattern usually thought to have been devised by Greatbatch is the so-called 'pineapple and basket' motif. Found on salt-glazed stoneware pieces as well as on lead-glazed earthenwares, it can be seen on a sauceboat and a teapot in these two bodies respectively (Fig. 5). However, it seems that there were a number of variations on

Figure 3 Salt-glazed stoneware 'blocks' from which master moulds were taken for the body of a teapot and for spouts, attributed to William Greatbatch of Fenton, *c.* 1755–60, and discovered at the Wedgwood factory in the early 20th century. Cauliflower shapes were used for many different Staffordshire tablewares. H. of teapot block 4¾ in (12 cm). Courtesy Josiah Wedgwood and Sons Ltd.

Figure 4 Lead-glazed earthenware cauliflower-moulded teapot and cover, the lower part with a green glaze, the upper decorated with cream slip. The 'block' from which the mould for a teapot of this form was made is shown in Fig. 3. Orders for cauliflower ware are preserved amongst the Wedgwood papers. Staffordshire, *c.* 1755–65. H. 4⅜ in (11.1 cm). Presented by A. W. Franks Esq., 1887.

this pattern, so it can still only be attributed to Greatbatch. The teapot was probably made by Josiah Wedgwood on account of its brilliant glazes.

An earthenware body, often somewhat coarse in texture, was frequently used for moulded lead-glazed pieces. Many of these were made in the shape of fruit or vegetables, perhaps influenced by continental fashions, and were glazed in yellow

and green. Wedgwood's first contribution to the improvement of the product was an especially brilliant green glaze developed whilst he was associated with Whieldon and which had been perfected by 25 March 1759. The formula can be found in the 'Experiment Book'. The first royal order was fulfilled in 1765 when Wedgwood supplied 'a complete sett of tea things, with a gold ground and raised flowers upon it in green', an order which he believed no one else would undertake. The order came in June 1765, and the following month Josiah sent a box of samples to Queen Charlotte for approval, as he mentions in a letter to his brother dated 6 July 1765. By 1767 he had titled himself 'Potter to Her Majesty'.[1]

The British Museum collection includes examples of most types of pottery that were in production in Staffordshire in the 1750s and 60s. As it was not then general practice for them to be marked by their maker, the majority cannot be attributed with any certainty to a particular potter. These include the popular tortoise-shell and agate wares. Agate was made of different coloured clays mixed together, whilst tortoise-shell (referred to in the eighteenth century as 'cloudy' or 'mottled') was merely decorated with coloured glazes applied in the form of powdered metal oxides, then covered with a clear lead glaze. A fine earthenware body was used, and many pieces, such as teapots of shell shape, were slip-cast.[2] Some items in the collection, however, are known to have been the kind of piece that Wedgwood was making at the Ivy House and Brick House works. A magnificent green-glazed wall-vase in the shape of a cornucopia moulded on one side with a head of Flora symbolising Plenty within an asymmetrical-shaped cartouche and with tiny flowers at the upper end and a vine trail at the foot (Pl. 1) is usually attributed to Wedgwood. The rich colour of the glaze is always associated with him, and the 'block' for this vase is traditionally thought to have been modelled by William Greatbatch. Surviving bills show that he actually supplied such vases to Wedgwood ready for glazing, but this was presumably during periods when Josiah could not make enough to fulfil demand.

Two pieces in the Chinese style, particularly favoured during the rococo period between about 1755 and 1775, are likely to have been modelled by Greatbatch, perhaps even made by him, then glazed by Wedgwood. A teapot of hexagonal

Figure 5 Lead-glazed earthenware teapot and cover (*left*) with pineapple-and-basket moulding, decorated with green and yellow glazes, attributed to Josiah Wedgwood in partnership with Thomas Whieldon. Total H. 5 in (12.7 cm). Bequeathed by F. W. Smith Esq., 1923. Salt-glazed stoneware sauceboat (*right*), similar moulding, pattern attributed to William Greatbatch, Staffordshire, *c.* 1760. H. 2¾ in (7.1 cm). Presented by B. J. Harland Esq., 1919.

section and a tea-caddy, both decorated with strongly coloured yellow and green glazes, are constructed of rectangular pieces of clay with fairly thin walls moulded with Chinese figures. The edges of the walls have been joined together using water, the handle and spout and upper part being joined to the body of the teapot in the same way (Fig. 6). A charming sauceboat (Fig. 6) moulded with tiny flowers and with a foxglove motif was inspired by the shapes of silver sauceboats. It has a wavy outline which is typically rococo in feeling. Delicate green, yellow and grey glazes endow this piece with especial charm.

At this period Josiah made use of pot merchants elsewhere to market his pieces. Liverpool was an important centre for both distribution and export, and here the potter dealt with John Sadler (1720–89) and Guy Green (retired 1799) who were in partnership from 1761. In addition to selling pots manufactured by Wedgwood, they also developed a transfer-printing process for use on pottery. Some controversy still surrounds the precise nature of the technique used, but in general terms the process involved several stages.[3] A copper plate was first engraved with the scene to be reproduced. This was a specialist task carried out on a contract basis usually, in the 1760s and 1770s, outside the factory. The copper plate was inked and then wiped over to remove surplus ink. A piece of paper was next applied to the copper and the image inked on to it. The paper was then applied to the glazed pot and the image transferred to it. Finally, the pieces were fired. A collection of documents deposited at Keele University, Staffordshire, sheds considerable light on Wedgwood's Liverpool business connections.[4] The papers show heavy demand for pots, give prices and types sold, and reveal some of the problems that beset the trade at that time. The earliest surviving communication, dated 14 August 1762, from Guy Green, informs us of what articles were being sent to Liverpool for sale and reveals that Josiah was inclined to charge high prices for high-quality goods: '. . . I cannot help remarking that you charge your Plates, Bowls and Spoon Trays considerably dearer than the Blue and White Potters; they only charging a Gallon Bowl at 1.s/. and the rest proportionably lower. Pray what is the difficulty you find in making them? I dare say you have your Work cheaper done, and I am sure a great deal neater.'

Figure 6 Lead-glazed earthenwares with moulded decoration: (*left*) sauceboat with foxglove moulding, green, yellow and grey glazes. H. $3\frac{1}{2}$ in (8.8 cm); (*centre*) tea-caddy with chinoiserie scenes, pattern attributed to William Greatbatch, *c.* 1763, green, yellow, brown and grey glazes. H. $5\frac{1}{8}$ in (13 cm); (*right*) teapot, similar scenes, yellow, brown and green glazes, cabbage-moulded handle and spout. H. $5\frac{1}{8}$ in (13 cm). All made in Staffordshire, *c.* 1760–5. Presented by A. W. Franks Esq.

John Sadler asked for a decision on prices to be charged in a letter to Josiah Wedgwood of 26 January 1763. He writes that he would have discussed the matter with the potter in person but had missed him, and requests a list of wholesale and retail prices. By March the matter appears to have been settled, but there was a more serious development when Josiah lowered his prices in early 1764. On 18 February Sadler wrote: '. . . as to printing them any cheaper it is not possible. Consider 24 Bowls 5 subjects on each, firing and Loss, and Expence of Plates [i.e. copper plates on which the engravers, who charged high prices and required prompt payment, put the design for printing], which last Article we do not rightly know ourselves and think what is left for Labour!' In August Sadler was content enough to write 'We think you have fixt the Prices very well, and I am sure there will never be any Occasion to lower them in our Time; for I believe what will be sold by you, and by us, will be as much as we can do.' The constant calls by Sadler and Green for more ware would appear to bear this out. A letter of 19 March 1763 contains this request:

Desire you'll send as soon as possible some Enamell'd Cream Colour, Flowers for the Warehouse, as under.

> 24 Quart Coffee Pots
> 12 Pint D⁰ ———
> 48 Large Size Tea Pot
> 96 Middle Size D⁰ ———
> 48 Small D⁰ ———
> 24 18′ Milk Jug
> 24 24′ D⁰ ———
> 24 Slop Bowls ———
> 24 Sugar Bowls and Covers

The list gives a typical range of pieces that found a ready sale at this time. By the end of the decade a number of new shapes were on sale such as 'silver pattern sallads', 'oval compotiers' (square and octagonal ones also appear in the correspondence), 'twiflers' (small plates), 'cushion comports' and 'sweetmeat baskets'. 'Pickle leaves' were first mentioned in an account dated 16 May 1769, and it is likely that the example in the British Museum, which is partly gilded, dates from this period (Fig. 7). It is especially light in weight and is made of a very pale cream-coloured earthenware. The glaze is thinly applied and has pooled to show

Figure 7 Creamware moulded 'pickle leaf', partly gilt, *c.* 1769, mark WEDGWOOD. L. 7⅝ in (19.4 cm). Presented by A. W. Franks Esq.

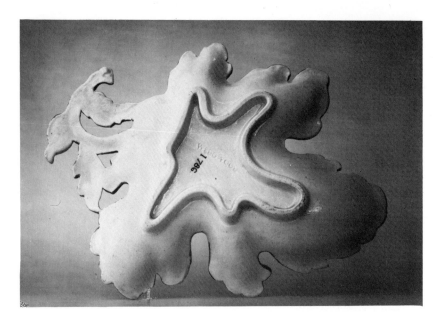

Figure 8 Reverse of 'pickle leaf' (Fig. 7) showing mark.

its faint greenish tinge only on the underside beneath the somewhat prominent foot. The mark on the underside of this piece (Fig. 8) is a large form usually found on pieces which exhibit the characteristics associated with the early period of creamware manufacture.

In a letter of 6 October 1764 (Mosley 1431) John Sadler commented on one of Josiah Wedgwood's most noteworthy achievements in the technical sphere. Wedgwood had been producing creamware since at least 1761. He was by no means the first Staffordshire potter to do so: for instance, in the British Museum is a bowl bearing the date 1743 and the initials EB, probably for Enoch Booth of Tunstall.[5] It was, however, Wedgwood's research that led to the manufacture of a considerably refined body. On 6 October 1764 Sadler wrote to him in approving terms: 'We have unpackt the 18 Crates we recd. and the Ware is very good. It is of a paler Colour, in general, which is lik'd vastly better by every Body than the deep Yellow, and will be better in every Respect. We like the Dishes much, they are very tasty; and very shortly you shall see them grand Things . . .'

We know from a letter of 1768[6] that Wedgwood was unable to produce both the deep and the pale cream-coloured earthenware concurrently, which means that the colour of the body can be taken as a guide to dating. The improvement appears from Josiah Wedgwood's notebooks, preserved at the Wedgwood factory, to have resulted from fritting (or melting and grinding) the glaze ingredients in order to avoid crazing. Creamware is in fact composed of the same materials as fine white stoneware, although it is covered with a lead, rather than a salt, glaze and fired at a lower temperature. In 1763 Josiah called his cream-coloured earthenware[7] 'a species of earthenware for the table, quite new in its appearance, covered with a rich and brilliant glaze bearing sudden alterations of heat and cold, manufactured with ease and expedition, and consequently cheap having every requisite for the purpose intended'. It was with creamware that he laid the foundations of his large fortune and for the continued prosperity of the firm bearing his name. The body has been in constant production ever since.

Over the years Sadler and Green voiced various complaints and compliments to Josiah Wedgwood. Not long after the beginning of the association between the

Liverppol firm and the Burslem pottery, which seems to date from December 1761 on the evidence of a surviving account for expenses incurred for the transport of pottery, Guy Green wrote to Wedgwood on 31 March 1763 (Mosley 1431) in a most complimentary vein: 'Was this Day favour'd with your's – As to the shape of your Tea Pots I think they will never be mended – They are the best Shape for shewing Heads, or any other subject, that can be, and the shape is often particularly commended. The last parcel of lids is also quite elegant; They rise a little something like a Coffeepot Lid, which gives an agreeable Appearance to the Whole.'

Not all Sadler and Green's comments were as favourable, and from time to time mishaps occurred, as we learn from a note to an account of 13 December 1770: '*Sir*, The Carrier [presumably Daniel Morris, or a member of his family, as they seem to have done a great deal of business with Sadler and Green], left Crate N.60. containing the Dishes, and another, last journey at Warrington, and they came yesterday, so thoroughly soaked with Rain, that I am apprehensive of great damage in firing.'

At least some of the pieces sent from Burslem must have been glazed at Liverpool as well as printed. In a letter of 27 March 1763 to Thomas Wedgwood Sadler asked for mugs 'of your best Biscuit – we are for trying a White Glaze, w.ch may be of Advantage'. When requesting '12 three pint Bottles & Basons' and other items on 25 April 1769, Guy Green wrote 'Pray let these be of a good shape, not too thick at bottom, nor thin on the Edge; for when the Edges are thin the glaze does not stick on'. A large part of the work of the Liverpool concern was, however, to print on Wedgwood ware, mainly on cream-coloured earthenware. Red and black printing was being carried out by June 1764, if not earlier, and on 26 May the correspondence mentions 'a new Colour a kind of dark Purple . . . as glossy and fine as possible'. It was probably not produced in quantity until 1770, when on 25 April Sadler wrote: 'We rec'd your's, and have made several Essays towards a Purple Colour some Time ago, but find it very difficult – We shall not however give it up – If you can give us any Hint should be oblig'd to you.'

Two plates in the British Museum of cream-coloured earthenware printed in lilac with two men in a landscape with ruins have elaborately pierced rims with feather-edge moulding and are therefore likely to date from around 1770, since pierced plates are mentioned in a letter of 4 October 1770 (Fig. 9). The plates cost 8*s* 6*d* the dozen (presumably the charge made for printing) and were 'Bt of Sadler and Green' by Josiah Wedgwood. The same scene is printed in black on a slightly larger plate in the Museum, its plain lobed edge decorated with black-printed flower sprays. It is impressed WEDGWOOD and has two other incised marks which are probably workman's marks.[8]

The black-printed version of this scene is not uncommon, but the lilac print is much more rarely found. The subject was the work of Robert Sayer who published the *Ruins of Athens with Remains and other Valuable Antiquities in Greece* in 1759.[9] Sayer admits in his preface that he had taken the work of J. D. Le Roy, *Les Ruines des Plus Beaux Monuments de la Grèce*, published at Paris in the previous year, 'properly arranging the subjects' and reducing the number of plates by half in order to 'accommodate the students in this art'. Some alterations were made when the print was adapted for transfer-printing on to Wedgwood's creamware as part of the temple structure has been omitted, together with figures on the bridge, whilst a stump and foliage have been added.

Not all the patterns are mentioned by name in the correspondence of Sadler and Green with Josiah Wedgwood. Some which do occur are 'Bute's Head' (2 August 1763), 'Harvest Home' (May 1763), 'Masons Arms' (September 1763), 'Red Birds' (mentioned as late as 12 December 1782), black flowers on shell-edged ware, green shells, purple landscape, purple birds, black landscape and

Figure 9 Creamware plate with pierced and feather-moulded rim, impressed 'Wedgwood', printed with 'Corinthian Ruins' pattern representing the Temple of Pola in Istria in lilac by John Sadler and Guy Green at Liverpool, *c.* 1770. The stylised flowers are painted. Diam. 9 in (23 cm). Presented by Mr and Mrs Isaac Falcke, 1909.

green flowers (all invoiced in November 1782).[10] Shells printed in black and hand-coloured in green are found on three plates, two of creamware (Fig. 10)[11] and one of a whiter crazed fabric.

Four creamware plates of lobed outline are decorated in iron-red with square prints obviously intended for tiles (Pl. 3) and often found on them. Depicting scenes from Aesop's *Fables*, these prints do not appear to be mentioned in the Sadler correspondence with Wedgwood (on loan to Keele University). The subjects, although not uncommon on tiles usually dated to the early 1770s, are extremely rare on plates. The 'Hunted Beaver' (Fable LXII) derives from a wood engraving by Samuel Croxall in his 1722 edition of the *Fables*; the 'Cock and the Fox' (Fable XXVII) is based on the same book, as is the 'Old Hound' (Fable XXVIII); and the 'Lark and her Young Ones' (Fable XXXVIII) has probably been adapted from the illustration in Croxall, with the addition of a tree in the centre and a landscape scene on the right. The plates must have been part of a series, but in view of the differing impressed factory marks they were presumably made at different times. However, they could still have been decorated as a group after being sent to Liverpool. The 'Hunted Beaver' and the 'Cock and the Fox' are impressed Wedgwood; the other two have the mark in small capital letters. Incised marks on all but the 'Cock and Fox' plate were probably made by the workmen responsible for moulding the plates.

It cannot be ruled out that the plates were decorated with these printed subjects either as an experiment or perhaps even by mistake. So far the only others which have come to light are twelve in the Schreiber Collection presented to the Victoria and Albert Museum in 1884. Purchased abroad in 1877, they all

depict differing Fable subjects, except for one which has a biblical theme; but none correspond with the plates in the British Museum.[12] In general Wedgwood tablewares printed at Liverpool do not have any additional painted decoration such as the green festoons on these Fable plates, since this added considerably to the cost of production. It may well be, therefore, that they represent a special order. They have not yet been traced in surviving documents, or perhaps the documents have disappeared. They are likely to have been made about 1775 on the basis of the similarity of their decoration to that found on Liverpool tiles already mentioned, and by virtue of their neoclassical festoons. The plates show a typically English blend of the neoclassical and the rococo. Their hexafoil shape, the scattered flowers on their borders and the scrolled elaboration of the frame around the lively painted scenes are in marked contrast to the severe neoclassical husk motif.

The British Museum collection contains several other examples of printed creamware apart from those already mentioned. The punch pot, or large teapot (Fig. 11), is printed with Masonic symbols. It has the cabbage-moulded handle and spout associated with the Wedgwood factory but is made of an inferior body to the pieces already mentioned. The extensive crazing which has become stained probably marks it as one of Josiah's earlier products, on the premise that the improvements made by the potter led to the disappearance of such faults. The dull appearance of the surface of the pot also points to a date of manufacture before the development of a brilliant glaze for creamware. The design incorporating the protractor and other mathematical instruments, below the motto DEUM TIME ET REGEM HONORA ('Fear God and honour the King'), is known on a pierced silver jewel dated 1766,[13] and may well have been in use before this date.

There is also a tea-caddy (lacking its lid) moulded in two parts and printed in black with, on one side, an early version of the design known as the 'Tea Party No 1' (Fig. 12) and, on the other side, a design known as 'The Shepherd'.[14] According to Cyril Cook, this was printed in red on a creamware coffee-pot inscribed 'R.H. 1767' and marked 'Wedgwood',[15] and can therefore be confidently attributed to the engraver Robert Hancock, although the precise source of

Figure 10 Creamware plates with shell-edge moulded rims outlined in green impressed 'Wedgwood' (*left*) and WEDGWOOD (*right*); printed in black, with shells, including a pecten or scallop shell (*centre left*) and a nassa snail shell (*top right*), and seaweed hand-coloured in emerald green. Printed by John Sadler and Guy Green at Liverpool, *c.* 1770–80. Diam. $7\frac{5}{8}$ in (19.4 cm). Presented by Mr and Mrs Isaac Falcke, 1909.

the scene still remains unknown, for it doubtless originally came from a painting. Hancock, who was born around 1729 or 1730, was a prolific engraver who moved from the Battersea Enamel Works in London to the Worcester porcelain factory. Later he was associated with the Caughley works, then went to Birmingham and London, dying at Brislington near Bristol in 1817. The Museum tea-caddy has a large incised cross on the glazed base and is impressed WEDGWOOD. It was probably printed in Liverpool around 1767 and is fairly heavy for its size with a pale body. Of similar colouring is a small saucer (Fig. 13) with rococo moulded decoration based on shell forms with the remains of gilt decoration on the edge of the moulding. The cup of matching pattern (Fig. 13) with crossed-ribbon handles, their terminals partly gilt, is slightly lighter in tone but has the same impressed mark as the saucer – 'wedgwood' – and is likely to have been made during the same period. Both have incised marks, probably made by the workmen responsible for making them, and are printed in black with long-tailed birds, a favourite motif on pottery and porcelain in the mid-eighteenth century. These birds resemble, but are not identical with, engravings published by Sayer in 1762 intended for copying on to various objects from furniture to metal trays by amateur lady painters.

Figure 11 Creamware punch pot and cover with cabbage-moulded handle and spout, unmarked but attributed to Josiah Wedgwood on the grounds of its shape; printed in black with the arms of the Premier Grand Lodge of the Order of Freemasons by John Sadler and Guy Green at Liverpool, c. 1764. H. 7 in (17.8 cm).

Domestic creamware has been the mainstay of the Wedgwood factory over a long period: the forerunner of present-day tablewares, it is still in production. Examples of hand-painted creamwares in the British Museum collection are discussed in Chapter 4, together with another category of earthenware which Josiah called 'pearl white', generally now called 'pearlware' (see also Chapter 7). Although associated with the end of the eighteenth century, it was first developed by Josiah Wedgwood in 1779, and was the culmination of work in progress since 1765 on a material which would have the appearance, if not the qualities, of porcelain. Richard Champion still held the monopoly for Cornish china clay, an essential ingredient for the manufacture of true (or 'hard-paste') porcelain. The original patent granted in 1768 to William Cookworthy was purchased by Champion who applied for an extension of its term in 1774. Josiah Wedgwood came into conflict with Champion but eventually compromised by using a Cornish

Figure 12 Creamware tea-caddy (cover missing) printed in black with a version of the design known as 'Tea Party no. 1', impressed WEDGWOOD and incised cross, *c.* 1767. Printed by John Sadler and Guy Green at Liverpool. H. $5\frac{1}{8}$ in (13.1 cm). Presented by A. D. Passmore Esq., 1957.

Figure 13 Creamware cup and saucer with rococo moulding, remains of gilding on edge, impressed 'Wedgwood' on both with incised workmens' marks; printed in black with long-tailed birds by John Sadler and Guy Green at Liverpool, *c.* 1761–7. Diam. of saucer 4⅛ in (12.3 cm). Presented by William Edkins Esq., 1887.

china clay in a pottery body. The pearlware composition required a higher firing temperature so that fuel costs, as well as the costs of transporting the clay, meant that pearlware was more expensive to produce than creamware.

After working with Thomas Whieldon at Fenton where he began experimenting with glazes whilst producing common pottery in various bodies, Josiah then went on to manufacture pottery on his own account. The partnership he established in 1766 with his cousin Thomas owed its prosperity to the refined creamware body developed by Josiah and used for a wide variety of domestic articles. Royal patronage, first obtained by the fulfilment of an order in 1765, ensured the success of this body, often referred to after 1767 as 'Queen's ware'. However, the name of Josiah Wedgwood probably remains best known for his unglazed stonewares, chiefly those made in black basalt and his famous blue jasper ware. These were produced initially during the Wedgwood and Bentley ornamental partnership and are the subject of Chapter 2.

2 Wedgwood and Bentley and the 'ornamental' partnership

Josiah Wedgwood first met Thomas Bentley (1730–80), his future partner in the Ornamental Branch of the pottery business, in 1762. At that time Bentley was a merchant in Liverpool. Originally from Derbyshire, he had been well educated and had also travelled in Europe. It was on a visit to Liverpool that Wedgwood sustained an injury to his already diseased right knee, which was eventually to be amputated. During his enforced stay there he came into contact with Bentley through his doctor, Matthew Turner. The two men became correspondents, and within a few years Bentley was acting as Wedgwood's agent in Liverpool, as we know from a letter from Wedgwood of 26 June 1766.[1] The potter tried hard to persuade Bentley to become his partner, the original idea being that he should live in Staffordshire on the Ridgehouse Estate purchased by the potter in July 1766. This, however, was not an appealing prospect to Bentley, who was active in Liverpool's religious and social affairs. A Proposal drawn up in November 1767 (Mosley 1826) shows what Josiah had in mind:

Warrington Novr 15,. 1767

Resolved

That W & B do enter into Partnership in making ornamental Earthenware or Porcelain viz Vases, Figures, Flowerpots, Toylet Furniture and such other Articles as they shall from Time to Time agree upon. The partnership to continue for the space of 14 years.

That J W shall build a dwelling House for T B for which T B shall pay 7 p^{er} C^t for the money laid out in building the said House for 14 yrs certain, & likewise a set of Workhouses for which the C^o shall pay 7p^r C^t for so much as they shall cost building. J W shall advance the money necessary to carry out the s^d business, for which he shall be paid 5 p^r Ct by the Company.

The full agreement between the two men was not signed until 10 August 1769, although the new works had opened on 13 June 1769. Bentley seems never to have lived in the house intended for him in Burslem, for in August 1769 he moved to London permanently, where he was in charge of the showroom and the decorating workshops. In June 1767 John Wedgwood, Josiah's older brother, had died by drowning in the Thames after a visit to the Ranelagh Gardens in Chelsea. This not only caused the potter acute grief but also deprived him of his London agent, so Thomas Bentley filled a much-needed role as a salesman and seems to have been skilful in predicting what kinds of ornamental wares would meet the demands of an increasingly fashionable clientele.

Josiah appears to have been keen to charge the highest prices for his productions that the market would bear, and he had certainly acquired a substantial fortune by the time of his death in 1795. His will, preserved amongst the Wedgwood papers deposited at Keele University in Staffordshire,[2] reveals that he was worth about £250,000 at the end of his life. The following carefully calculated statement appears at the end of the section pertaining to Class xx in the first

Wedgwood and Bentley catalogue issued in 1773; this class was made up of 'Tablets for Chimney Pieces; and Pictures for Cabinets and inlaying, upon Plates of the artificial Basaltes, and upon a new Kind of enamelled Plates':

> . . . the *Price* of these Paintings depends upon so many Circumstances, attending the Execution, that it is not easy to give any satisfactory Idea of it in Writing. It varies according to the Size of the Plates; the Number of Figures, the Merit of the Hands employed, and the *Degrees* of *finishing*. All Persons are sensible that Works of great *Risque* and *Expence* cannot be executed without being sold for proportionte Prices; and in this Instance the Artists can truly say they have the *smallest Profit* upon their *highest Works.*

There is no doubt that Josiah had exceptional flair for business: even in the early days he realised the necessity of bold expansion. We know from a letter he wrote to Bentley on 18 July 1766[3] that he bought the Ridgehouse Estate for £3,000. This was the site of his new pottery which he named Etruria. Nothing demonstrates more clearly than this choice of name the firm's commitment to the new taste for domestic articles in the classical manner. Moreover, the potter was most sanguine in his hopes of making profits from his schemes of expansion, and from the partnership which he was pressing Bentley to join in November 1767.

As is clear from a profit and loss account which has fortunately survived amongst the Wedgwood papers, the first years of the partnership were promising. The account covers the period 10 August 1769 to 31 December 1775[4] and shows that the 'Goods on Hand' in the first year were valued at £1,086 10s 5½d. Manufacturing and selling expenses amounted to £1,920 15s 9¼d, and goods sold came to £2,404 5s 3¾d. The years 1773 and 1774 were the most profitable with the highest figures for goods sold. The final figures given at 31 December 1775 show that the total turnover reached the astonishing figure of £25,228 3s 7d during the period. Nearly £2,000 were spent on 'Models & Model Molds. Books. Prints. Buildings & Fixtures &c'. A surviving list of books with their prices made out by Josiah Wedgwood in August 1770[5] shows that he believed in investing in sourcebooks to provide him with new shapes and decorative motifs. He went so far as to pay 18 guineas for six volumes of *Antiquities of Herculaneum*[6] and £18 for fifteen volumes of Montfaucon's *L'Antiquité Expliquée.*[7] A close examination of his vases, which were the chief vehicles of the partnership's originality as well as the source of a large part of its profits, reveals a startling variety and inventiveness.

CREAMWARE

At first, just as the useful partnership was largely based on creamware, so too the ornamental partnership used creamware for vases, which were in production until at least the time of Thomas Bentley's death in 1780. During this period the partnership was constantly thinking of new decorative finishes which would meet with the approval of its customers. Plain creamware vases were being made before the beginning of the partnership. They were mentioned in a letter from Josiah to his brother John dated 6 July 1765 (E.25-18080) concerning the commissions for Queen Charlotte: 'I shall be very proud of the honour of sending a box of patterns to the Queen, amongst which I intend sending two setts of Vases, Creamcolour, engine-turned, and printed . . .' A small number of examples have survived, including an engine-turned garniture of three vases at Saltram House, Devon.[8] In the British Museum is a creamware vase decorated with a pale caramel- or buff-coloured slip. Its Greek-key pattern and pendent swags have been covered with a lead glaze (Fig. 14). Impressed 'Wedgwood & Bentley', it is a most unusual piece. This mark was probably used from about June 1773, when Josiah wrote to

Figure 14 Creamware vase decorated with buff-coloured slip, and a Greek key motif and swags in relief; impressed Wedgwood & Bentley, 1769–80. H. 7½ in (19 cm). Presented by Mr and Mrs Isaac Falcke, 1909.

his partner (see letter quoted on p. 36) that he had been ordering metal stamps, until shortly after Thomas Bentley's death in 1780.

The commonest ornamental creamwares are those decorated with various glazes imitating naturally occurring semi-precious stones, including agate, porphyry, various marbles and fine-grained stones like granite. According to the 1773 catalogue, the vases were sold in pairs, or sets of three, five or even seven pieces. The taste for classical antiquities had been taken up by the English milords, and Wedgwood's production represented a cheap version of the classical vases within the means of the gentry who aped the nobility. They were even cheaper than the blue-john (Derbyshire fluorspar) vases mounted in gilt-bronze by Matthew Boulton of Soho, Birmingham, who was anxious to supply mounts for Wedgwood's vases too. However, Josiah saw the flaw in this idea – his vases would probably not have been enhanced by gilt-bronze mounts – so he decided to use simple gilt handles and relief ornaments instead. Many of the variegated pieces were closely based on classical antiquities as interpreted by Jacques Stella, whose *Livre de Vases* was published by his sister Claudine with etchings by his niece Françoise Bouzonnet Stella before 1667.[9] A pair of somewhat idiosyncratic vases and covers with 'monster' handles and a bird (perhaps an eagle) and two chicks as the finials to the covers are clearly based on this source (Fig. 15). The handles, of plain creamware which has been gilded, were cleverly adapted from a vase by Stella in a volume of engravings owned by Josiah Wedgwood and Thomas Bentley (Fig. 16).[10] The vases are made of different coloured clays wedged together before the pots were thrown so that the colour, which is mainly red in tone, is in the clay itself and not just on the surface. To our eyes these vases may

Figure 15 Pair of 'agate' earthenware vases and covers made of different coloured clays with gilded monster handles and bird finials; white biscuit (unglazed) earthenware bases; mark Wedgwood & Bentley, 1769–80. H. 9$\frac{1}{8}$ in (23.3 cm).

28

look strangely inelegant, but they seem to have found a ready sale to the aristocrats and gentlefolk to whom they were so cleverly marketed.

Even before the beginning of the partnership Wedgwood seems to have been conscious of the possibility of selling items to people on the principle that they were fashionable with the very highest classes of society. In an undated letter to Bentley, perhaps written in September 1767 (E.25-18167), Wedgwood thanks him for sending off green and gold earthenware from Liverpool to the New World (it would no longer sell at home), and then remarks on the popularity of creamware:

> The demand for this said *Creamcolour*, Alias *Queens Ware*, Alias *Ivory* still increases. It is really amazing how rapidly the use of it has spread allmost over the whole Globe, and how universally it is liked. How much of this general use and estimation is owing to the mode of its introduction – and how much to its real utility and beauty? are questions in which we may be a good deal interested for the government of our future Conduct . . . The reasons are too obvious to be longer dwelt upon. For instance, if a Royal or Noble introduction be as necessary to the sale of an Article *of Luxury*, as real Elegance and beauty, then the Manufacturer, if he consults his own interest will bestow as much pains, and expence too if necessary, in gaining the former of these advantages, as he would in bestowing the latter.

Later, on 23 August 1772 (E.25-18392), during the period of intense production of vases Wedgwood wrote to Bentley:

> The Great People have had their Vases in their Palaces long enough for them to be seen & admir'd by the *Middling Class* of People, which we know are vastly, I had said almost infinitely, superior in number, to the Great, & though a *great price* was, I believe, at first necessary to make the Vases esteemed *Ornaments for Palaces* that reason no longer exists. Their character is established, & the middling People would probably buy quantitys of them at a reduced price . . .

Figure 16 Engraving from Stella's *Second Livre de Vases*, published in 1667, numbered 26, showing the source for the unusual handles on the vases in Fig. 15. From a copy of the book in the Victoria and Albert Museum.

In the same letter he mentioned that the firm now had upwards of 100 good forms of vases, with their moulds, handles and ornaments. In December he wrote angrily to Bentley (E.25-18427) that a Mr Ward, his agent in Bath, had advertised in the papers and was going to deliver handbills at the Pump Room, Bath, on behalf of the pottery. Wedgwood was not impressed by these manoeuvres:

> We have hitherto appeared in a very different light to common shopkeepers, but this step, in my opinion, will sink us exceedingly. I suppose these hand bills are publish'd in our names, as coming immediately from us. – Do you know what they are? I own myself alarmed at this step, & have wrote to Mr. Ward to desire he would not deliver any more hand bills coming from us, it being a mode of advertiseing [sic] I never approv'd of, & if they are printed in our names I think either you or I should have seen the advertisement before it was thus deliver'd.

The attention Josiah Wedgwood gave to the correct promotion of his products paid off. Even though we know from his letters to Bentley that he was not above 'doctoring' faulty vases and providing them with painted wooden bases or with ornaments in painted composition when their original ones had been damaged in firing, the firm did not lose custom. He made continual efforts to extend his markets: his plans in August 1770 included Dublin and Bath, both centres of fashionable life, where he thought he would be able to sell a large number of vases. Soon after, the potter received 'some excellent instructions for our Dublin plan' from Bentley and in turn sent him on 20 August a sort of memorandum (E.25-18318) entitled 'New means of exciteing attention to our Vases':

> Wo^d. you advertise the next season as the Silk mercers in Pell Mell do – Or deliver cards at the houses of the Nobility & Gentry, & in the City – Get leave to make a shew of his Majestys service for a month, & ornament the Desert with ornamental Ewers, flower baskets & Vases – Or have an Auction at Cobbs room of Statues, Bassreliefs, Pictures, Tripods, Candalabras, Lamps, Potpouri's, superb Ewers, Cisterns, Tablets Etruscan, Porphyrys & other Articles not yet exposed to sale. – Make a great route of advertising this Auction, & at the same time mention our rooms in Newport St., & have another Auction in the full season at Bath of such things as we have now on hand, just sprinkled over with a few new articles to give them an air of novelty to any of our customers who may see them there. – Or will you trust to a new disposition of the Rooms with the new articles we shall have to put into them & a few modest puffs in the Papers from some of our friends such as I am told there has been one lately in Lloyds chronicle – or something, but I have not seen it, & do not know the particulars.

An early letter of Wedgwood to Bentley dated 5 August 1767 (E.25-18161) reveals his almost boundless optimism for the future, as well as his scientific temperament which was to be the well-spring of his success.

> I am going on with my experiments upon various Earths, Clays &c. for different bodys, & shall next go upon Glazes. Many of my experiments turn out to my wishes, & convince me more and more, of the extensive Capability of our Manufacture for further improvements. It is at present (comparatively) in a rude, uncultivated state, & may easily be polished, & bro^t to much greater perfection – Such a revolution, I believe, is at hand; you must assist in, proffitt [sic] by it.

The profits were to come in the early 1770s when a veritable 'vase madness' broke out. It started with the vases imitating precious stones and continued with the more elegantly conceived vases of the first unglazed coloured stoneware to be made by the partnership, black basalt.

The creamware vases in the British Museum collection are amongst the greatest glories of Wedgwood's production. Their precise dating is not easy, yet some seem to display certain characteristics which suggest a date of manufacture or at least of design early in the existence of the partnership. One of these is the largest and handsomest of the Museum examples (Fig. 17). Its shape is somewhat impractical since it rests on a small cylindrical support rising from the circular foot which is only about 3 in (7.7 cm) in diameter and is therefore undeniably top-

Figure 17 Creamware vase and cover decorated with coloured slips in dark brown, red-brown, cream and green imitating marble; with gilded acanthus swag, 'sibyl' finial and handles with acanthus-leaf terminals; white biscuit (unglazed) earthenware base, mark Wedgwood & Bentley, c. 1773–80. H. 14¼ in (36.5 cm).

31

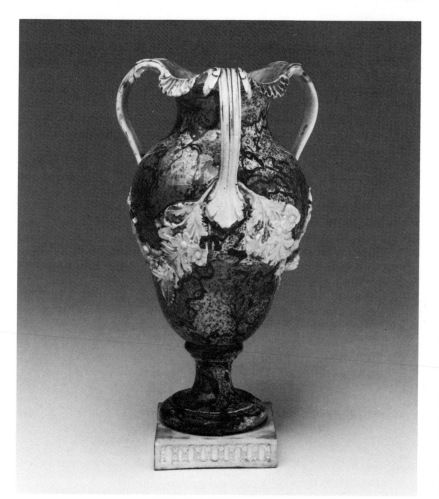

Figure 18 Creamware vase or 'three-handled flowerpot' decorated with ground-up cobalt oxide sprinkled on to the unglazed surface, splashed with cream slip and painted in black under the clear glaze so that the surface imitates agate; handles and flower swags covered with a clear lead glaze; white biscuit (unglazed) earthenware base, mark Wedgwood & Bentley, 1769–80. H. incl. base 7½ in (19 cm).

heavy. The base, also of earthenware, is unglazed. The 'sibyl' finial surmounting the lid is one of Josiah's own inventions and was introduced about 1773–4. The 'sibyl', a classically derived figure, never has the attributes of the biblical 'widow' who is traditionally shown with a cruse of oil and a barrel of meal. The first securely datable 'sibyl' finial is found on the ice pails made for the Imperial Russian dinner service delivered by Wedgwood in 1774.[11]

A much smaller vase with three handles, its surface once again decorated to imitate a coloured stone, is of more sensible proportions (Fig. 18). This vase, which appears in Wedgwood's accounts as early as 25 February 1769, was known in the eighteenth century as a 'three-handled flowerpot' and was kept in production for at least a decade.[12] Its wavy lip, which has a frilled edge, its curving handles, its flower reliefs which are draped over the body of the vase, itself of undulating outline, are all highly expressive of the rococo style which abhorred the symmetrical.

A ewer of marbled creamware imitating agate is in a contrasting style, although it was in production during the same period (Fig. 19). The ovoid-shaped body is entirely regular and has a suitably proportioned foot. The form actually corresponds to one being made in soft-paste porcelain by that home of highly sophisticated productions, the Chelsea-Derby factory.[13] Josiah Wedgwood commented in a letter to Bentley[14] on the showy nature of the Derby factory's procelain, so perhaps the sombreness of the dark-coloured surface of his ewer was a conscious attempt to provide a wholly different interpretation of their unknown common source. The relief ornament on the Wedgwood earthenware vase is probably of the factory's own devising and is quite different from the porcelain version. A thickly gilt Dionysian mask handle terminal and the laurel leaf and berry motif moulded on the handle and in relief around the upper part of the body are in a severely classical style.[15]

Vases seem from contemporary evidence, such as the catalogues produced by Wedgwood and Bentley, to have been sold in sets of seven, five or three. Two small vases with gilt goat-horn handles terminating in masks are beautifully decorated to imitate agate (Pl. 2b) and almost certainly formed part of a larger set. The shape

Figure 19 Creamware vase decorated with brown and cream slips, gilded satyr-mask handle terminal and a band of gilded laurel leaf and berry ornament; white biscuit (unglazed) earthenware base; impressed 'Wedgwood & Bentley', *c.* 1773–80. H. 10¾ in (27.3 cm).

is based on an etching by Marie-Thérèse Reboul Vien (1729–1805) in *Suite de Vases Composée dans le Goût de l'Antique* published in Paris in 1760 after designs by her husband, the painter Joseph Marie Vien (1716–1809).[16] The design was copied by Wedgwood and Bentley as their 'Number 1 shape', and examples first appeared in agate and marbled creamware around 1769. A number of variations were manufactured. A basalt vase of rather similar shape but with the addition of festoons appears in the painting of 1780 by George Stubbs, *The Wedgwood Family in the grounds of Etruria Hall*, now in the Wedgwood Museum, Barlaston. There is a much larger version of these vases, measuring 12 in (30.5 cm) in height, also in the collection,[17] and it is not unreasonable to speculate that different sizes of the same model were put together to make a set. These garnitures were intended for display on mantelpieces in the houses of the aristocracy or upper bourgeoisie.

Perhaps the most elegant of the creamware vases in the British Museum collection, and the only one which does not imitate agate, is a small vase and cover with a speckled blue-green surface imitating granite (Pl. 2b). The gilt ram's-head handle terminals fold over at the rim of the vase to form a bizarre small cherub head repeated on both sides of the handle. The motif is almost unnoticeable except when seen at close quarters, so flattened are the features of the heads. Similar heads can be seen on two black basalt vases, one marked WEDGWOOD & BENTLEY.[18] The motif probably derives from a vase illustrated in the first volume of Hamilton's *Antiquities*.[19] The circular base is attached to a square black basalt plinth with a brass screw secured by two circular washers, and the circular wafer marked WEDGWOOD & BENTLEY ETRURIA in relief in capital letters is on a raised circular pad pierced by the bolt already mentioned. This vase was exhibited at the National Exhibition of Works of Art held at Leeds in 1868. The original pink label printed in black is still attached to the inner surface of the lid of the vase.

Figure 20 Base of creamware teapot with decoration imitating agate (see Pl. 2a; for technique see Fig. 18) showing impressed 'Wedgwood & Bentley' mark, *c.* 1771. Diam. to edge of foot rim $3\frac{3}{8}$ in (8.5 cm). Presented by C. B. Farmer Esq., 1905.

A small teapot with decoration imitating a natural stone (Pl. 2a) can be assigned to the period between the commencement of the partnership and around November 1771. Although a 'useful' rather than an 'ornamental' production, it bears the Wedgwood and Bentley mark (Fig. 20). On 3 September 1770 Wedgwood wrote to Bentley (E.25-18324) defining the difference between the two categories manufactured by his useful and ornamental partnerships, specifically mentioning teapots as an obvious case where the line could be easily drawn. Josiah arrived at a rule which he thought could be applied without much trouble: 'May not usefull ware be comprehended under this simple definition, of such vessels as are *made use of at meals*.' This teapot is an article of extreme rarity; even its shape is untypical of useful wares made at Burslem or elsewhere in Staffordshire at this time. Its decoration, however, is so similar in technique and general appearance to the vases already described that it prompts the theory that it was perhaps an experiment. In a letter of 2 November 1771 (W/M 1441) Wedgwood wrote to Bentley:

> We have packed some Pebble Coffeepots, T.pot, sug.ᵣˢ and Cream Ewers, but they are too like the Agat [*sic*] pottery which has been made before & you will see by these specimens that it is the *forms* more than the *colours* of many of the Vases which has raised & unvulgariz'd them – Make exactly the same pebbles into Tea ware & they are let down to the Class of common Pott ware again, many degrees below *Queens ware* – Some of the things now sent may be rais'd again by tipping them with burnt in Gold . . .

It is possible that the British Museum teapot formed part of this consignment. It is worth noting that it has been in the Museum since 1905, when it was presented by C. B. Farmer Esq.

BLACK BASALT

The first stoneware to be used by the Wedgwood and Bentley partnership for ornamental purposes was the fine-grained black composition known as basalt from 1773 and referred to earlier than this as 'Etruscan'. For many years it has been supposed that basalt represented a refinement by Wedgwood of an existing body which had been in production in Staffordshire since the early years of the eighteenth century. The Elers brothers were thought to have made it, although there is no evidence that they ever did so. Josiah Wedgwood gave John Philip Elers no credit for it when discussing his work in a letter to Bentley,[20] although he mentioned the red ware made by this potter.

In 1910 one writer[21] investigated all the evidence for an early origin of the manufacture of black stoneware in England. He was unable to come to any firm conclusion regarding the dating of a teapot which has come to be considered as a key piece. This curiously modelled basalt pot in the British Museum[22] is shaped like a tree-trunk strewn with lichen. Impressed ASTBURY, it is now thought on stylistic grounds to have been made not by John Astbury, a potter who died in 1768, but at the end of the eighteenth century by Richard Meir Astbury, his son. The finial, which has not yet been securely dated, is of an unusual type. Disregarding the head which has been crudely restored, the draped seated figure surmounting the lid is probably a representation of Britannia since there is a shield at its left side crudely incised to represent the Union Jack. The lid exhibits the same characteristics as the rest of the pot and certainly belongs with it as the opening to the pot is irregularly shaped. The fact that this teapot has an impressed mark presumably stamped with a metal die indicates, but does not prove, a late-eighteenth-century date of manufacture. It seems that such impressed marks incorporating the names of potters were uncommon before the 1770s. If this late date for the Astbury teapot is accepted, then there is a distinct possibility that Josiah Wedgwood was after all the inventor of black basalt, although it must be admitted he never claimed credit for this invention.

Two other points are relevant to this discussion of the early origins of black basalt. In a recent exhibition catalogue[23] the view is expressed that black stonewares may have been made by Whieldon at the Fenton Low pottery, perhaps whilst Josiah Wedgwood was still working there; but no sherds have been excavated from this site which can be securely dated to between 1749 and 1759.[24] Josiah Wedgwood's notebooks[25] show that he was experimenting with local deposits of iron-rich Etruria marls and with black-band ironstone from Chesterton and elsewhere as early as 1759.

In a letter from Josiah Wedgwood to Thomas Bentley dated 29 August 1770 (E.25-18322) the potter points out that Thomas Wedgwood had 'bestow'd a great deal of attention for some time past upon China bodys [sic] for T: pots in brown, black, grey &c.'. However, even if black stoneware had been used experimentally at Burslem for useful wares, it found its most popular use for ornamental vases manufactured at Etruria. The first black basalt vases were sold in the summer of 1768. Basalt was chosen for the so-called 'First Day's Vases', six of which were made on 13 June 1769 and thrown by Josiah himself to inaugurate the Etruria factory which had been specially constructed for the ornamental partnership. Only four survived the firing process. Two can be seen at the Wedgwood Museum, Barlaston. Early black basalt pieces have a polished appearance and are silky to the touch. In the catalogue issued by the firm in 1773 the composition is described as 'A fine *black Porcelain* having nearly the same Properties as the *Basaltes*, resisting the Attacks of Acids; being a Touch-stone to Copper, Silver and Gold, and equal in Hardness to Agate or Porphyry'. Wedgwood had been careful to write to William Cox, the manager of his London showroom, on

Figure 21 Black basalt intaglio of a heart and anchor and the inscription ESPERE EN VOUS, impressed WEDGWOOD 411, late 18th century. H. ¾ in (1.9 cm). Presented by A. W. Franks Esq.

Figure 22 Black basalt intaglios; (*top*) lioness, unmarked, late 18th century. H. ¾ in (1.9 cm); (*centre*) squirrel, impressed Wedgwood & Bentley, 1773–80. H. ⅞ in (2.2 cm); (*bottom*) elephant unmarked, late 18th century. H. 1 in (2.6 cm). All presented by A. W. Franks Esq.

31 August 1768 (E.96-17667), 'NB the polish is natural to the Composition and is given in burning [in firing], they are never oiled &c.'.

A category of black basalt pieces that proved extremely popular was Class I in the 1773 catalogue, the cameos and intaglios. As the catalogue states, they were taken from the finest antique gems and were intended for rings and bracelets, for inlaying in cabinets, writing tables, bookcases and other pieces of furniture; the intaglios were used as seals, and collections of both cameos and intaglios could be made at moderate expense. The potter stressed the desirability of his cameos and intaglios by mentioning how he had managed to obtain a large number of subjects: 'By the Favour of the Nobility, &c. who are in Possession of original Gems, or fine Impressions of those in foreign Collections, we have been enabled to make our List pretty numerous.'

The British Museum collection of intaglios is made up of over 200 basalt specimens with both antique and modern subjects which were catalogued by R. L. Hobson in 1903.[26] All were presented by A. W. Franks with additional jasper intaglios; twenty-five jasper examples were added by Mr and Mrs Isaac Falcke in 1909. A fine example of the basalt intaglio (No. 115) depicting Julius Caesar and Livia bears the 'Wedgwood & Bentley' impressed mark (see below). The subject is listed in the firm's catalogue issued in 1774. This intaglio, unlike most in the Museum collection, is set in a gold fob seal. It forms part of the Hull Grundy Gift to the British Museum and is discussed and illustrated in a forthcoming publication.[27]

Amongst the 'modern' subjects, which mainly consist of portraits of royalty and famous persons, are a few with sentimental subjects. One is an intaglio of a heart and anchor with the French motto ESPERE EN VOUS (Fig. 21), probably best translated as 'My hope is in you'. The subject, numbered 441, is not in the catalogue of 1787 and must have been introduced at the end of the century or even at the beginning of the nineteenth century. Intaglios of a squirrel, a lioness and an elephant (Fig. 22) are a reminder of the continuing popularity of animal subjects, especially in England. The squirrel and elephant are listed in the catalogue of 1787 as Nos 386 and 387 in Class I, Section II, showing that they were 'modern subjects'; they may have been based on the work of a contemporary gem-carver. The lioness, however, is listed as an 'antique subject' and is No. 57 in the same catalogue.[28] The intaglio of the squirrel is impressed Wedgwood & Bentley. This gem would appear to have been made after June 1773, for on 21 June (E.25-18474) Wedgwood wrote to his partner: 'I shew'd his Grace [the Duke of Bridgewater] a couple of polish'd seals, which he admir'd greatly, & said they were very fine things. The seal Engravers were to be pitied as Men whose business was at an end.' He concludes the letter by saying 'I have been buying some small Types, & ordering a still smaller stamp cut with *Wedgwood & Bentley* to mark our seals with.'

A double-sided intaglio (Fig. 23) in the British Museum has on the obverse a scene depicting the greatest actor of the day, David Garrick (1717–79) looking into the face of Shakespeare with the legend QUO ME RAPIS TUI PLENUM ('Where are you carrying me away to, filled with your spirit?' is a possible translation) and MARCHANT F. It is after a gem by Nathaniel Marchant (1739–1816), a famous English contemporary gem-cutter and medallist whose work is represented by a number of engraved gems in the collection.[29] The reverse has a bust of Cleopatra to the right, another Shakespearean subject. A second intaglio is signed HARRIS for William Harris, a rather obscure gem-cutter known to have been working around 1788, when he was at the Royal Academy, and 1792. It shows a profile head to the left, probably representing George Washington (Fig. 23), doubtless for the export market, and is impressed WEDGWOOD.

Two unmarked oval basalt plaques with relief scenes enclosed within a moulded frame with crossed ribbons (Figs 24, 25) are said to be amongst the

Figure 23 Black basalt intaglios: (*top*) head of David Garrick (1717–79) looking into the face of Shakespeare, inscribed QUO ME RAPIS TUI PLENUM, signed MARCHANT F for the gem-cutter Nathaniel Marchant (1739–1816), unmarked, late 18th century. H. ¾ in (2 cm); (*bottom*) head of George Washington (1732–99), signed HARRIS for the gem-cutter William Harris (fl. 1788–92), impressed WEDGWOOD, late 18th century. H. ⅞ in (2.35 cm). Both presented by A. W. Franks Esq.

Figure 24 Black basalt plaque with scene moulded in relief of 'The War of Jupiter and the Titans' after della Porta, within integral moulded frame; unmarked, by Josiah Wedgwood and Thomas Bentley, *c.* 1773. L. 9⅞ in (25 cm). Presented by Major-General A. Meyrick, 1878.

Figure 25 Black basalt plaque with scene moulded in relief of 'The Feast of the Gods' after della Porta; unmarked, by Josiah Wedgwood and Thomas Bentley, *c.* 1773. L. 10 in (25.5 cm). Presented by Major-General A. Meyrick, 1878.

earliest pieces of black stoneware made by Wedgwood. One authority[30] traces the source of these stories from Ovid to metal plaquettes by the Italian Renaissance sculptor Gugliemo della Porta (died at Rome 1577) aided by a Flemish craftsman, Jacopo Cobaert, and they are thought to have been made between 1550 and 1575. It is not known how or from whom Wedgwood and Bentley obtained an example of the plaquettes, for the potter does not refer to it in any of his surviving letters. However, these classically inspired subjects probably had fashionable appeal in the early 1770s when neoclassical taste began to prevail in cultivated circles. That the powerful modelling of the nude forms depicted in typical heavily muscled style by della Porta can be distinguished in these low-relief basalt plaques is a

37

considerable technical achievement on the part of the potter. The subjects are listed in Class II as No. 2, 'The War of Jupiter and the Titans', and No. 4, 'The Feast of the Gods', in the 1773 catalogue, and the format given as oval measuring 9 by 6 in (23 × 15 cm). Both types are of some rarity. It seems from the explanation prefixing the list of subjects that the plaques were intended to take the place of pictures for putting on walls. On 8 January 1775 (E.25-18582) Wedgwood wrote to his partner: 'I think it impossible for us to make any frames of pottery, however fine or coloured, that will not degrade the gem or picture.' A rectangular basalt plaque showing a Bacchanalian Sacrifice is illustrated elsewhere.[31]

Difficulties in firing basalt satisfactorily were still being experienced even in August 1770, as Wedgwood explained to Bentley (E.25-18316):

> It is impossible to make the surface of the black Vases allways alike, the difference being made in the fire, a little more or a little less, a little quicker, or a little slower makes the difference. The last as you observe are the roughest we have had of a long time, oweing [sic] merely to their having a little too much & too quick a fire. But I am trying another method to render the surface smoother in general when no accidents happen in the fireing [sic], which is to burnish them when they are pretty hard, with steel burnishers, 'till they have the polish of a mirror; but as this is done by hand, it is very tedious work, but they take an admirable polish if the fire does not destroy it, which I can acquaint you of soon, having sent one of them to Burslem to be bisketed there.

This shows that these vases were polished before firing when they were in the so-called 'cheese hard' state. The same method is used today.

Amongst the finest of the black basalt vases in the British Museum is a vase with elaborate snake handles. On one side is a scene in relief of the Muse Erato and her lyre with a cupid holding a wreath in front of her (Pl. 6b). The neck and foot are vertically engine-turned. The foot rests on a square basalt plinth impressed Wedgwood & Bentley twice on the underside. The surface of the vase glows with an almost coal-like intensity. A number of basalt pieces were decorated with painting in the so-called 'encaustic' technique, and these are discussed in Chapter 4.

Three pieces of black basalt which required the skill of the plaster maker and modeller serve to introduce us to the work of the most important English sculptor commissioned by Wedgwood. John Flaxman jun. (1755–1826) is acknowledged as being one of the most talented of all British sculptors.[32] The length of his association with Wedgwood and the amount of work he executed distinguish him from all the other practitioners of the art. These included Lochée and de Vaere, who were employed to model portrait medallions (see pp. 70, 71), Webber, whose most outstanding contribution was the modelling of the scenes on the Portland Vase (see p. 118), and the group of little-known Italian sculptors such as Angelo Dalmazzoni (dates unknown), Camillo Pacetti (1758–1826), Angelino Fratoddi (dates unknown) and Giuseppe Angelini (1742–1811), who worked in Rome for Wedgwood under the direction of Flaxman.[33]

John Flaxman Sen. (1726–95) was one of a number of plaster makers in London who supplied the partnership with models and casts, usually but not always copies from classical, French or Italian sources. He was connected with Wedgwood and Bentley in 1771 or earlier on the evidence of a letter written by the potter to Bentley on 16 February of that year (W/M 1441):

> I wrote to you in my last concerning busts. I suppose those at the [Royal] Academy are less hackney'd & better in General than the Plaisters [sic] shop can furnish us with; besides it will sound better to say – This is from the Academy, taken from an Original in the Gallery of &c &c – then to say, we had it from Flaxman.

An invoice of 25 March 1775 (L.I-204) records that Flaxman Sen. supplied models for 'A pair of vases one with a Satyr & the other with a Triton Handle £3.3'. The plasters are preserved at the Wedgwood Museum and may be based

Figure 26 Black basalt ewers, 'Sacred to Neptune' (*left*) and 'Sacred to Bacchus' (*right*), based on a plaster model supplied by John Flaxman Sen. in 1775, impressed WEDGWOOD AND BENTLEY ETRURIA in relief within a circular wafer; on water ewer (*left*) the mark is on a pad of clay placed on the underside of the plinth, 1775–80. H. water ewer 15¼ in (38.6 cm), wine ewer 15⅛ in (38.4 cm). Presented by Mr and Mrs Isaac Falcke, 1909.

on a French source by Claude Michel, called Clodion (1738–1814), a sculptor best known for his terracotta figures and bas reliefs.[34] The basalt vases are known as the 'wine and water ewers' or the ewers 'Sacred to Bacchus' and 'Sacred to Neptune' (Fig. 26), the satyr symbolising wine, and the triton riding on a dolphin representing water. They are amongst the most elaborately modelled pieces ever produced by the Wedgwood factory. Both bear the WEDGWOOD & BENTLEY mark which occurs in an unusual form on the water ewer (Fig. 27). The shape was popular during the eighteenth and nineteenth centuries in various materials including silver and even malachite.[35] The Wedgwood vases were made in jasper ware in the late eighteenth century, and in majolica (lead-glazed earthenware) and bone china in the nineteenth century.

John Flaxman jun. was an undeniably precocious young artist in his teens when Wedgwood first heard of him. He is presented in a somewhat unflattering light in a rather gossipy letter written by Wedgwood to Bentley in September 1771.[36] Wedgwood recounts that there was 'company' at the works almost every day, and that recently a Sir George Strickland with his wife and father-in-law, a 'Mr Freeman of Schute Lodge in Wilts', as well as her two brothers, had visited the factory. According to Wedgwood, this Mr Freeman, a man of taste, 'is a great admirer of young Flaxman & has advised his Father to send him to Rome which he has promised to do. Mr Freeman says he knows young Flaxman is a Coxcomb, but does not think him a bit the worse for it *or the less likely to be a great Artist*'. However, it is clear that the boy was gifted with unusual ability. He exhibited at the Free Society of Artists as early as 1767-8 and received a silver medal for pieces exhibited at the Royal Academy in 1770 when he was aged fifteen. Before long his character seems to have improved, as Josiah wrote to Thomas Bentley in January 1775 (E.25-18583): 'I am glad you have met with a Modeler & that Flaxman is so valuable an Artist. It is but a few years since he was a most supreme Coxcomb, but a little more experience may have cured him of that foible.'

A basalt bust of Mercury (Fig. 28) is likely to have been modelled by Flaxman jun. not long after the death of Thomas Bentley. However, the piece does not represent any departure in style from the range of busts produced by the partnership. The sculptor exhibited a bust of Mercury at the Royal Academy in 1781, and offered a cast of Mercury to Wedgwood in the following year[37] which was probably of this version of the bust. Wedgwood had also ordered a 'Mercury' from the plaster makers Hoskins and Grant in 1779 (without specifying whether it was a full-length figure or a bust), and this has led to some uncertainty over the attribution of the basalt piece. The subject was a popular one, undoubtedly based on a classical prototype, and is probably distantly related to a marble which was first recorded in 1536 in the statue court of the Belvedere, Rome, and has been in the Uffizi, Florence, since at least 1734 when it appeared in Gori's *Museum Florentinum*,[38] a copy of which Wedgwood owned. However, despite having two plaster models of Mercury, the firm does not appear to have actually issued a bust of the winged messenger of the gods during the eighteenth century, or at least until after 1789, as it is not listed in any of their catalogues.

One of the most unusual objects based on an Antique bronze is a rare vase in the shape of a human head produced in black basalt. The example in the British Museum (Fig. 29) has traces of the bronzing so often associated with the early products of the ornamental partnership, although in fact it continued in use much later than the 1770s.

The 'bronzing' process for basalt, together with that for 'encaustic' painting (see p. 88) was the only one ever patented by Wedgwood. Taken out in November 1769, the patent was soon withdrawn. From a study of Wedgwood's notebooks it is clear that the bronze effect was achieved by dissolving pure gold in *aqua regia* (a mixture of nitric and hydrochloric acids, able to dissolve gold and platinum),

Figure 27 Mark on pad of clay on black basalt water ewer (Fig. 26).

Figure 28 Black basalt bust of Mercury, impressed 'Wedgwood', modelled by John Flaxman jun., *c.* 1782. H. incl. base 20 in (51 cm). Presented by Mr and Mrs Isaac Falcke, 1909.

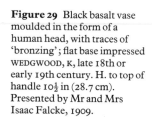

Figure 29 Black basalt vase moulded in the form of a human head, with traces of 'bronzing'; flat base impressed WEDGWOOD, K, late 18th or early 19th century. H. to top of handle $10\frac{1}{2}$ in (28.7 cm). Presented by Mr and Mrs Isaac Falcke, 1909.

precipitating it by copper, drying and carefully storing it for some time (in powder form), mixing it with turpentine and applying it to the almost-dried ware which was burnished after firing.[39] Wedgwood originally called the ware 'Bronze Etruscan', but altered the name in 1773, when his first catalogue appeared, to 'Bronze Basaltes'. Examples of bronzed basalt are rare.

The vase has been claimed to derive directly from a bronze in the Louvre,[40] but the story may be more complicated than that. The Etruscan bronze in the Louvre was acquired only at the beginning of the nineteenth century, although it had been excavated at an unknown date by Prince Aldobrandini from Gabii, a site in the vicinity of Rome which was despoiled by Gavin Hamilton in 1792. However, a seventeenth-century drawing of a very similar bronze commissioned by the antiquarian Cassiano dal Pozzo[41] is known (see Fig. 30), and it could have been accessible through some printed reproduction which has not yet been identified. There was a copy of the Louvre bronze in the collection of the connoisseur Richard Payne Knight (it is uncertain whether it was thought to be an original during the owner's lifetime); the location of this copy cannot be accurately ascertained until 1824 when it entered the British Museum collection.[42]

The basalt vase is illustrated in the 'first shapes book' kept at the Wedgwood factory as 'Shape No 196'; this is a Victorian compilation that cannot be used as a guide to the dating of the model. At the time it was drawn up a black basalt example $11\frac{1}{2}$ in (29.2 cm) high cost 21s. The Museum version measures only $10\frac{1}{2}$ in (26.7 cm) in height. The impressed mark on the flat base of the basalt head in large capital letters and the presence of a fairly noticeable seamline (where the two parts of the moulded piece were joined) are not infallible indications of a nineteenth-century date, but make the author inclined towards a date of manufacture in the early years of the nineteenth century even though it could have been modelled earlier. The significance of the impressed mark K is still uncertain: it has been said to be a workman's mark used by William Keeling (fl. 1763–90), but as yet no evidence has been found to connect him with this piece. The history of the Museum vase can be traced back only as far as an exhibition held at Crystal Palace, London, in 1856 where it was displayed, according to an inscription in indelible pencil on the flat base.

One of the most remarkable and mysterious pieces in the British Museum collection and one which falls outside the dates of the partnership is a basalt tray with a silver inlay (Fig. 31). It was illustrated by Captain Grant[43] beside a footed bowl and cover from his own collection, 5 in (12.7 cm) in height and unmarked. He attributed this piece to the Wedgwood factory, it seems, on the grounds of the decoration, also in silver, which closely paralleled the egg-and-dart motif on the Museum tray. The present writer does not know the current whereabouts of the bowl and cover. A fluted sugar bowl and cover surmounted by a 'widow' finial and a cream ewer with a similar cover are illustrated in a publication of 1898,[44] and formed part of a service which also included a teapot and a bowl. The basalt is decorated in silver with a stylised tongue pattern. These pieces were in a private collection and may perhaps have belonged with the Museum tray, which was exhibited at the Crystal Palace in 1856, in 1862 at the Art Treasures exhibition, in Leeds in 1868 and at Bethnal Green in 1875.

Despite repeated efforts to discover the origin of the unusual decoration of the tray, no documents have yet been found that refer to it. There is a possibility, but no proof, that it was made during the period when Josiah's gifted son Thomas was working on the development of photography using silver. In preparation for a paper which he read before the Royal Society on 10 May 1792 on the 'Production of Light and Heat',[45] Thomas Wedgwood carried out a series of experiments using cream-coloured earthenware cylinders, coated with silver and polished, which were prepared for him at the factory. Documents on loan to Keele Univer-

Vaso, che, servia neli sagrifiti: antichi

Figure 30 Drawing of a vase in the form of a head mounted in a volume of items commissioned by the antiquarian Cassiano dal Pozzo (1588–1657), inscribed 'Vaso, che, servia neli sagrifiti: antichi' ('vase which served for ancient sacrifices'). The drawing was bought from the Albani Collection by King George III. Copyright reserved. Reproduced by gracious permission of Her Majesty the Queen.

Figure 31 Black basalt tray decorated with silver inlay of scattered stylised flowers and an egg-and-dart motif; impressed WEDGWOOD, probably *c.* 1791. L. 12¼ in (31.2 cm). Presented by Mr and Mrs Isaac Falcke, 1909.

sity shed some light on his work[46] but little on the Museum tray. However, a letter of February 1791 (E.25-17650) from Josiah Wedgwood to Thomas Byerley, manager of the London showroom, contains the tantalising words 'The silvered ware you will soon see – You say you want some thing – Just mention what articles we shoud [*sic*] attempt & we will exert ourselves to furnish you with them –'.

CANEWARE

A 'dry body', or unglazed composition fired at a slightly lower temperature than a true stoneware, which was used at the Wedgwood factory as a basis for encaustic decoration (see p. 97), is known as caneware from its resemblance to bamboo cane. Although, like the basalt body, it has been kept in production over a long period of time, it has always been produced in lesser quantity than basalt. It is usually pale yellow in tone (although it can vary to a deeper shade) and is non-porous. Its composition was given in Josiah Wedgwood's own 'Experiment Book'[46a] as:

> 20 parts Purbeck clay
> 4 red clay
> 5 calcined flint
> 3 alabaster
> $\frac{1}{2}$ limestone
> $\frac{1}{16}$ smalt [powdered glass of deep blue colour]

Various formulae were tried, and the body appears to have been a refinement of an existing iron-bearing buff body based upon local clays.

Caneware appeared for the first time in the catalogue of 1787 (seven years after Bentley's death), although it was being made from at least 1779. No pieces seem to have survived from the early 1770s, despite a reference to 'Fawn colour'd articles' in a letter from Wedgwood to his partner of 9 September 1771[47] and even earlier. The potter seems to have abandoned the 'tryals' he was making in November of that year, perhaps because all the pieces he made were apt to 'fly' or shatter when they came in contact with hot liquid. Even on 16 September 1779 (E.26-18923) Wedgwood was not entirely happy with the material, as he wrote to Bentley: 'Our present cane-colour body is very imperfect. It has a course [*sic*] speckled appearance if examined with attention. It being porous & apt to stain, I have not yet been able to give it a porcelain texture & preserve its colour, but if I live I hope to compass it.'

A caneware cup and saucer of pleasingly simple shape which have been turned on the lathe are two of the relatively few pieces of tableware in this material (Pl. 13). Both cup and saucer are impressed WEDGWOOD (the saucer has z also). A caneware figure of Voltaire made shortly before Bentley's death is discussed within the context of sculpture (see Chapter 3), and a vase decorated in the encaustic technique (both on Pl. 13) is discussed in Chapter 4.

The caneware and basalt medallion illustrated on Pl. 13 is an extremely rare piece. Only one other example, which belongs to the Wedgwood Museum, is known to the author. It shows a finely modelled supplicating negro slave in black on a cane-coloured ground with the impressed inscription AM I NOT A MAN AND A BROTHER, filled in with black, and was modelled in 1787 after the seal of the Slave Emancipation Society which was founded in that year. Wedgwood played an active part in the business of this society and was on its committee by February 1788. In this month he was busy with the affairs of the Society and sent some of his new small cameos of the same subject, also made for the Society, to Benjamin Franklin in America.[48]

The medallion is unusually constructed. Plaster has been used to fix the oval caneware plaque to the moulded basalt frame which is 1.5 cm ($\frac{5}{8}$ in) deep and 5 mm ($\frac{3}{16}$ in thick). The layer of plaster extends about 1.5 cm ($\frac{5}{8}$ in) leaving visible the irregular oval of the caneware plaque slightly smaller than the ground of the basalt relief. There is a hole in the top of the basalt frame for suspension, so the object was obviously not intended to be enclosed in a wood or metal frame, despite the rather crude finish of the reverse. Small black and white jasper medallions of this subject are much more common and were used as buttons or brooches (see p. 62–3).

'ROSSO ANTICO'

Wedgwood adapted the red ware manufactured in some quantity in Staffordshire since the time of John Philip Elers and which he himself made (see Fig. 1 for pieces attributed to him), and gave it the new name of '*rosso antico*' when using it for ornamental ware in the neoclassical idiom. He seems to have consented somewhat unwillingly to its use for anything except teapots on the grounds of its 'extreme vulgarity', as he wrote to Bentley in a letter of 10 March 1776 (E.25-18660): 'I will try to imitate the *Antico Rosso* from your description [Bentley had probably referred to Roman red pottery, or Samian ware, as it is often called], but when I have done my best I am afraid where one spectator thinks of *Antico Rosso* an hundred will be put in mind of a *Red Teapot*!' The British Museum collection has no examples of the ware from the partnership period. It includes some pieces which could have been made during Wedgwood's lifetime,[49] although '*rosso antico*' was certainly more popular with Josiah's son, Josiah II.

Wedgwood's greatest contribution to the composition of ceramic bodies, since it was completely original, was jasper ware, which is still in production and is invariably associated with his name. Jasper ware is a fine-grained stoneware, containing carbonate or sulphate of baryta, which is sometimes translucent. It can be stained with metal oxides to colour it and is most familiar in blue, which is obtained from cobalt oxide. In the early 1770s Wedgwood carried out a long series of experiments culminating in the creation of the new composition in 1774–5, although it was not perfected until 1775 and was still the subject of trials until the 1790s during the period leading up to the manufacture of the Portland Vase (see Chapter 6). The hundreds of surviving 'trials' preserved at the Wedgwood Museum, which are a small fraction of the original several thousand, reveal just how painstaking he was. His letters to Bentley show that he had a prolonged struggle with the problems of firing and colouring the body. From surviving cracked and blistered pieces we can see what sort of problems he encountered.

The earliest mention of experimental work relating to the new body occurs in a letter from Wedgwood to Bentley of 13 January 1771.[50] The potter wrote that he had been going through and making a general review of his experiments, writing up any that needed it. The first of his present projects was 'To make a white body, succeptible [sic] of being colour'd & which shall polish itself in burning Bisket'. In other words this was to be a vitrified body which needed no glaze. The new material had also to be capable of taking a stain. It was originally envisaged as a means of producing 'wonderfull pebbles', that is, variegated vases such as those mentioned earlier (p. oo), but in the event the potter's experiments were to carry him in a quite different direction.

By the end of 1772 he had still not perfected a new body for gems (cameos and intaglios), even though he wrote to Bentley on 31 December[51] that he had mixed bodies several times but had failed to achieve any satisfactory results. From a letter written a year later on 30 December[52] it is clear that white cameos (presumably of jasper) were being made. Mr Cox, the warehouseman, had sent some to Matthew Boulton, maker of ornamental metalwork in Soho, Birmingham, and Wedgwood was not pleased about this, as he had not been consulted. He was always plagued by imitators, who quickly put into production any new line that he had brought out, and jasper ware was to be no exception. The market was in any case in need of stimulation. Josiah felt that what was required in the early 1770s was a new material. It was only on 1 January 1775 (E.25-18578) that he was able to write to Bentley that he was 'absolute' in blue of almost any shade, and could also make 'a beautifull Sea Green, & several other colors, *for grounds to* Cameo's, Intaglio's, &c'; but he still had to conquer the problem of staining, as the colour from the ground was liable to spread to the white relief when they were fired together. All the labour did eventually pay off, and jasper ware became the best known of all Wedgwood products.

The British Museum houses one of the largest collections of jasper ware in the British Isles. Inevitably only a few outstanding pieces can be discussed here; some well-known productions in fact come within the scope of the next chapter which is devoted to portrait medallions. It should also be mentioned at this point that two vases, known as the Pegasus and Portland Vases, are given separate chapters (5 and 6) of their own, and do not date from the years of the partnership. All colours of jasper were manufactured in the eighteenth century (except for the extremely rare yellow) are represented in the Museum collection, as well as the various techniques of decoration such as engine-turning, application of finely finished reliefs, surface stippling and polishing on the lapidary wheel.

Flat pieces of jasper were made first. A strange white body, often with specks, which Josiah called his 'waxen composition', was probably the forerunner of jasper ware, although it bears little resemblance to the later white jasper body. It is perhaps closer to a type of stoneware made extensively in the first half of the nineteenth century and called 'smear-glazed stoneware', because it was very lightly glazed with salt, and is usually greyish or brownish in colour. Josiah's 'waxen' pieces (which are not glazed) do, however, have a 'fatty' texture, which other stonewares lack. A few items in the British Museum collection are made of this rare composition. An oval medallion within a metal frame representing Flora (Fig. 32) is based on an Antique statue of this subject in the Farnese Palace, and is illustrated in at least one of the books on classical antiquities which Josiah is known to have possessed and used as a source-book: it can be found on pl. LI of Maffei's *Raccolta di Statue Antiche e Moderne*, published at Rome in 1704.[53]

A circular medallion in the waxen composition modelled with the head of a Gorgon in extremely high relief is a masterpiece of the potter's art (Figs 33, 34). According to the firm's catalogue issued in 1787, the head was based on 'an exquisite marble in the possession of Sir W. Hamilton'.[54] These medallions were produced in several versions and are more common in blue jasper than in the waxen composition. It is not entirely clear which type Josiah is referring to in his letter to Bentley of 25 November 1776 (E.25-18719), but the letter helps to date the Museum medallion. He wrote: 'We will make no more Gorgons Heads – But these being some of the finest things we have, & not knowing they did not sell, we ventur'd to make a few more of them at a time when we did not know what to make.' However, it is worth remarking that the subject was in production at a much later date during the nineteenth century.

Figure 32 White jasper ware medallion of Flora moulded in relief in the 'waxen composition' within a metal frame; unmarked, by Josiah Wedgwood and Thomas Bentley, *c.* 1772–3. H. incl. frame 3⅜ in (8.7 cm). Presented by Mr and Mrs Isaac Falcke, 1909.

Figure 33 White jasper ware medallion of a Gorgon's head moulded in high relief in the 'waxen composition' within a metal frame; impressed WEDGWOOD & BENTLEY (see Fig. 34), *c.* 1772–3. Diam. 5¼ in (13.4 cm). Presented by Mr and Mrs Isaac Falcke, 1909.

Figure 34 Impressed WEDGWOOD & BENTLEY mark on reverse of white jasper ware medallion of Medusa. The octagonal hole allowed the escape of gases released during firing.

Some of the blue jasper ware plaques in the British Museum collection are very fine and have been singled out for special mention. A small oval plaque, presented by A. W. Franks, of grey-blue jasper with a metal frame has a relief of the well-known subject 'The Marriage of Cupid and Psyche' (Fig. 35) which is taken from a sardonyx cameo by Tryphon formerly in the collection of the Earl of Arundel. From its subsequent owner, the third Duke of Marlborough, in whose family it remained between 1780 and 1875, it took its name 'the Marlborough gem'. However, Wedgwood copied it from the rather inaccurate drawing by T. Netscher engraved by Bernard Picart for Stosch's *Pierres Antiques Gravées* of 1724,[55] an example of which Wedgwood owned in 1770.[56] The most notable feature is the lack of a wing on the right-hand cupid; the legs of the stool and the torch have also been taken from the engraving and differ from the gem. The front leg of the stool is now missing on the plaque. This immensely popular subject produced in several different versions at Wedgwood, including one adapted by John Flaxman jun., appears in truncated form on a hard-paste porcelain medallion from the Falcke Collection.[57] Made at the Berlin porcelain factory, it is signed by J. G. Kranich and dated 1789.

A solid grey-blue oval jasper plaque of Hercules and the Nemean lion (Fig. 36) is probably based on a gem subject frequently encountered in works illustrating antique gems from famous cabinets. The Labours of Hercules were widely represented in Renaissance works of art, and Wedgwood's plaque is very similar to a base metal plaquette in the Museum collection.[58] This is considered to be the work of an unidentified Italian artist (perhaps a goldsmith or a gem-cutter), using the pseudonym Moderno, who was active in the late fifteenth and early sixteenth century.[59] The Wedgwood plaque has been carefully tooled, and the fur of the lion is particularly well delineated.

Figure 35 Solid grey-blue jasper medallion with relief of the Marriage of Cupid and Psyche after the 'Marlborough Gem', a sardonyx cameo now in the Boston Museum of Fine Arts, USA, in metal frame, impressed WEDGWOOD & BENTLEY, *c.* 1774–80. L. incl. frame 3½ in (8.9 cm). Presented by Mr and Mrs Isaac Falcke, 1909.

Figure 36 Solid grey-blue jasper medallion with relief of Hercules and the Nemean Lion perhaps based on a Renaissance base metal plaquette by Moderno, impressed Wedgwood & Bentley, *c.* 1774–80. H. 3¼ in (8.3 cm). Presented by Mr and Mrs Isaac Falcke, 1909.

Two of the most interesting of all the pieces from the Wedgwood and Bentley era are a remarkable pair of pedestals which are amongst the only examples of jasper hollow ware made before Thomas Bentley's death (Figs 37, 38). The pedestals are shaped, having a flat square top, pierced by a circular hole, and flaring sides. On each corner of the pedestals is an applied strip of clay moulded with acanthus leaf and berry ornament with a ram's head at the top and a hoof at the bottom. On each side is a white jasper relief of a cupid symbolising one of the four seasons; the attributes are a brazier for Winter; a bird and a nest filled with eggs for Spring; a flower garland for Summer; and a scythe and a sheaf of corn for Autumn. These motifs are in fairly high relief and are well modelled. A band of interlaced circles, probably punched with a metal tool, ornaments the lower edge of each pedestal. However, although the decoration is well-thought out, the grey-blue jasper ware, apparently washed darker blue on the upper surface, is of poor quality. Each pedestal is blistered and fire-cracked, especially underneath where there are three small circular holes on each corner for the release of gases. These extremely unusual objects were probably intended as supports for figures.

An illustration of a white jasper crouching Venus on a rocky base of pale blue jasper attached to a blue and white pedestal with the same mark as the Museum examples has been published elsewhere.[60] The cupid symbolising Autumn is shown in a different attitude on that piece as he stands on a wheat-stalk and holds three stalks in his left hand, whereas on the Museum pedestal he stands on a piece of ground next to a shrub and has a sheaf of corn over his left shoulder. The pedestals could be merely misfired rejects but they could also be experimental pieces, the forerunners of the vases, ewers and teawares made in jasper ware after the death of Thomas Bentley.

THE LEGACY OF THE PARTNERSHIP YEARS:
JASPER IN THE LATE EIGHTEENTH CENTURY

A pair of magnificent blue jasper ware ewers of the *oinochoe* (Greek wine jar) form with serpent handles have a 'dimpled' surface (Fig. 39). This effect was produced by the use of a special tool or roulette wheel with a spiked attachment that ran over the surface of the leather-hard pot.[61] Although they were not made during the partnership period, the ewers are very much in the spirit of the Bentley years and utilise a form which had enjoyed great popularity in creamware in the 1770s. Their shape is far more common in creamware than in jasper, although the earthenware examples have different handles. These solid blue jasper ewers are ornamented with reliefs from the 'Maternity' series by Lady Templetown, one of a group of amateur lady artists whose designs were utilised by Wedgwood towards the end of the eighteenth century. Lady Elizabeth Templetown (1747–1823) first supplied designs in about 1783, as we know from a letter to her from Josiah Wedgwood[62] which states that he had completed the first bas-reliefs from her designs. Only two designs described as her work in the 1787 catalogue can be definitely associated with her: 'An Offering to Peace' and 'Friendship Consoling Affliction' based on a classical relief from the Albani Collection (now in the Louvre Museum, Paris);[63] whilst the 'Oven Books', or records of firings, record 'Templetown's Sporton Love', usually now known as 'Sportive Love', in July and August 1784.[64] Several others are usually attributed to her – 'The Bourbonnais Shepherd', 'Charlotte at the Tomb of Werther', 'Poor Maria' and 'Maternal Affection' being amongst them.

The same unusual dimpled surface can be found on a pair of vases for bulb growing (Fig. 40). Each has a detachable lid fitting on to a ledge inside the vase. Applied leaves decorating the lower part of the body and the foot conceal the join of the two parts. The top imitates rockery and is ornamented with applied flowers

Figure 37 Grey-blue jasper pedestals with darker blue wash on upper surface, ornamented with reliefs of cupids symbolising the four seasons: (*left*) winter and spring; (*right*) summer and autumn; impressed Wedgwood & Bentley, probably *c.* 1775–80. H. to top of pedestal 3⅛ in (8 cm). Presented by Mr and Mrs Isaac Falcke, 1909.

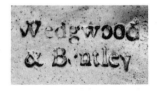

Figure 38 Impressed Wedgwood & Bentley mark on undersides of jasper ware pedestals (Fig. 37).

51

Figure 39 Pair of blue jasper
ewers of *oinochoe* form with
'dimpled' surfaces, ornamented
with reliefs from the
'Maternity' series by Lady
Templetown; impressed
WEDGWOOD, incised T, late 18th
century. H. (*left*) 10¾ in (27.3
cm); (*right*) 10⅝ in (27.1 cm).
Presented by Mr and Mrs
Isaac Falcke, 1909.

Figure 40 Blue jasper bulb
vase with three bulb holders
(one of a pair), the main part
'dimpled' or granulated,
ornamented with reliefs of the
Muses and trophies of the Arts;
impressed WEDGWOOD, V,
c. 1785–90. Total H. 8⅞ in
(22.7 cm).

in white jasper ware. Three bulb holders fit into three shaped holes in the lid. The body is decorated with reliefs of the Muses: on one side from left to right are Euterpe, with her double flute (lyric poetry), Clio holding a scroll (history) and Erato shown with a lyre (erotic poetry and mime); and on the other (Fig. 40) are Polyhymnia shown in a pensive attitude (sublime hymn), Terpischore with a lyre (dance and song) and Calliope with a tablet (epic poetry).

The Muses were a popular subject and at least one version was modelled for Josiah Wedgwood in early 1775 by John Flaxman jun., who supplied plaster casts, possibly on behalf of his father, completing the series himself a few months after the original delivery. It is likely that the original idea was adapted from an illustration of a sarcophagus in the Capitoline Museum, Rome, which can now be found in the Louvre, Paris.[65] It is shown in Joseph Spence's *Polymetis* published at London in 1747 (pl. XII). There is another 'dimpled' bulb pot in the Art Institute, Chicago.[66]

John Flaxman was also responsible for a famous set of chesspieces produced in various colours of jasper ware and modelled in 1783. A figure of a 'Fool for Chess' was invoiced to Wedgwood on 30 October 1783 at a cost of £1 5s.[67] It was intended for France where the Bishop is replaced by *Le Fou*. The wax figure preserved at the Wedgwood Museum was presumably the item referred to in the invoice. In early 1784 Wedgwood was expressing admiration for the chessmen, which are mentioned in the 'Oven Books' from December 1783.[68] Early examples seem to have had rudimentary, or in some cases flat, circular bases such as those shown in a highly finished drawing by Flaxman in the Wedgwood Museum for which the artist received £6 6s.[69] The sets themselves were sold for five guineas. Several figures have obvious mould lines, and it is difficult to believe

Figure 41 Solid grey-green jasper knight (*left*) from a chess set designed by John Flaxman jun. in 1783, impressed 'Wedgwood'. White fool (*right*) from the same set, intended for the French market, impressed 'Wedgwood', incised workman's mark. H. (*left*) 2¼ in (5.8 cm); (*right*) 2¾ in (7.1 cm). Both presented by Mr and Mrs Isaac Falcke, 1909.

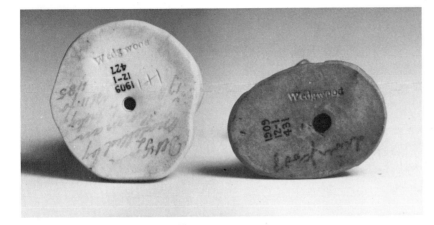

that Josiah I would not have insisted on a better finish. Nevertheless, all the chesspieces retain their detailed and vigorous modelling.

Sets of chessmen were produced in various colours. The pieces in the British Museum are white; white on lilac or green circular bases with white edges; a rather bright blue; muddy brown; grey-green; and green. A white king and queen, a blue queen and a green queen all have octagonal bases. Dating the Museum chesspieces is problematical, but it is likely that the majority were made long after Josiah I's death. Of particular interest is a white fool on a pad-shaped base of roughly circular outline (Fig. 41). A knight of solid grey-green jasper (Fig. 41) has a similar factory mark (Fig. 42), although it has no incised mark, and an oval pad-shaped base. It also has a hole in the base, but this is oval and slightly larger than that of the previous piece.

Amongst the rare sculptural pieces produced in jasper is a pair of candlesticks remarkable for their well-modelled figures of Ceres and Cybele (Fig. 43). Ceres, the goddess of the harvest, is shown with her emblem, a sheaf of corn, and Cybele, the goddess of agriculture, is accompanied by a lion. The design of these candlesticks has been attributed to John Flaxman but on stylistic grounds only. The combination of the figures with an over-large and elaborate candlestick-holder in the form of a cornucopia leaves much to be desired aethestically, but there is no doubt that these classical-style female figures are the work of an experienced modeller.

The name of the English architect Sir William Chambers (1726–96) occurs a number of times in Wedgwood's letters to his partner. A pair of griffin candlesticks in white jasper on blue plinths with blue jasper candleholders (Fig. 44) are related to a design by Chambers which appeared in the 1792 edition of his *Treatise on Civil Architecture*. The wooden block mould for the figure, which has been attributed to John Coward, is preserved at the Wedgwood Museum. Coward, a woodcarver of London, is reputed to have worked for the Adam brothers. It is presumed that the griffin candlestick was first produced in jasper a few years before Josiah's death, and the British Museum's examples probably date from this period. The huge wings of the griffin are remarkable for their careful tooling which can also be noted on the creature's head.

The small white jasper busts on blue jasper dip pedestals, themselves ornamented with trophies in relief, are a category that has not yet been fully studied. Four unusual pedestals supporting classical busts (Fig. 45) were probably made towards the end of the eighteenth century, and it is possible that they took their inspiration from Sèvres figures or busts on waisted pedestals, often known as *gaines* in France because of their characteristic waisted shape. They may derive

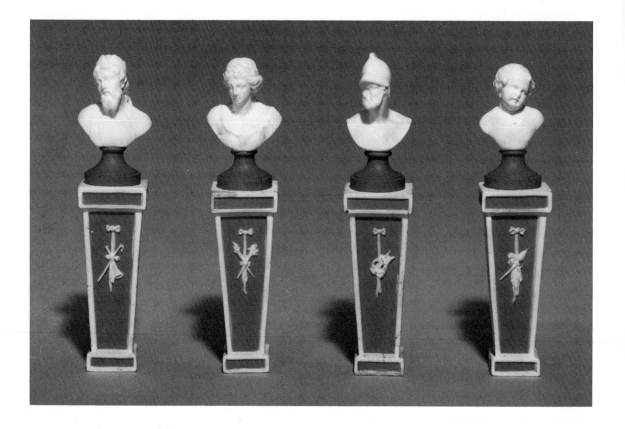

ultimately from classical term figures such as the bronze Jupiter shown in the third volume of Count Caylus's publication.[70] Some Continental factories, such as Fürstenberg, were also producing small busts of biscuit (that is, unglazed) porcelain on shaped pedestals. It is difficult to discover the purpose of the Wedgwood pieces: they seem insufficiently stable to stand alone as sculpture and may have been fitments to other objects or to a piece of furniture as they each have a circular hole extending almost all the way through the pedestal. So far only detached examples numbering fewer than a dozen have been noted in other collections.[71] However, there is a possibility that they correspond to the 'small busts with emblematical terms' listed in the catalogue produced by the firm in 1787. The reliefs on the British Museum pedestals are symbolic of love as they include crossed torches, a lyre and a wreath, a shepherd's crook and a lyre and a distaff, perhaps an emblem of domesticity. Most of the attributes were common as ornamental motifs at least as early as 1762 when they are mentioned in a French treatise on the use of precious stones.[72]

Josiah Wedgwood employed the technique of polishing his unglazed stone-wares on the lapidary wheel from an early stage. Jasper ware cameos and intaglios were made with bevelled edges and were sometimes of white jasper dipped in blue and the edges polished. A pair of drum-shaped salt cellars (Fig. 46) of solid blue jasper have a polished interior surface. This technique and the impressed mark suggest that they were manufactured in the last decade of Josiah Wedgwood's life. However, the reliefs which ornament the cellars were modelled considerably earlier and are the best-known of all John Flaxman jun.'s works for Wedgwood. The subject, known as the 'Dancing Hours', was probably taken from de Mont-

Figure 45 Four white jasper busts in classical style on blue jasper plinths attached to blue and white jasper pedestals ornamented with trophies of love, impressed 'Wedgwood' (*first and second left only*), late 18th century. H. of helmeted man 5¾ in (15 cm). Presented by A. W. Franks Esq.

Figure 46 Blue jasper dip salt cellar (one of a pair) with polished inner surface, decorated with applied reliefs of the 'Dancing Hours', first modelled by John Flaxman jun., *c.* 1778, impressed 'Wedgwood 3, S'. Diam. $3\frac{5}{16}$ in (8.4 cm). Presented by Mr and Mrs Isaac Falcke, 1909.

faucon's *L'Antiquité Expliquée*,[73] a copy of which Josiah owned in 1770,[74] and comes originally from a late Greek relief of the first or second century BC formerly in the Villa Borghese, Rome, and now in the Louvre, Paris.[75] The first reference to the subject in Wedgwood's correspondence occurs in an undated letter from him to Bentley of September 1776 (E.25-18696) on the subject of 'Bass relief Vases' in which he mentions a drawing 'you sent for plain Vases to paint, which we find likewise very suitable for Bass reliefs particularly for the Dancing Hours'. By April 1778 it is clear that he had used the figures for a 'tablet' or plaque intended for a chimneypiece.[76] It was subsequently used to ornament an extremely wide variety of pieces made at the Wedgwood factory. The salt cellars were evidently considered an admirable example of the potter's art well over 100 years ago as one has on the base a printed label from the National Exhibition of Works of Art held in Leeds in 1868.

The inner surfaces of many hollow pieces made at the end of the eighteenth century were polished for a more practical reason, since this improved their capacity to hold liquid. For instance, a pair of blue jasper wine-coolers (Fig. 47), which would have held water to maintain the low temperature of the wine bottles placed in them at a meal, have polished interiors. Measuring $8\frac{1}{2}$ in (21.4 cm) in diameter and bearing the mark WEDGWOOD, the coolers are ornamented with reliefs in white of Bacchanalian boys designed by Lady Diana Beauclerk (1724–1808) around 1783. Lady Diana Beauclerk supplied designs between 1783 and 1789, mainly of boys at play or carousing.[77] She was the daughter of the second Duke of Marlborough and, after the dissolution of her marriage to Lord Boling-broke, married the wit Topham Beauclerk. She obtained work from Wedgwood

in the first instance through the politician Charles James Fox, who apparently sent one of her designs to the potter. The group was used on plaques and medallions including one incorporated into a marble clock by Vulliamy (see p. 127).

Engine-turning was another decorative process used to great effect on teawares. Fluted and diced patterns could be achieved by cutting away a layer of coloured clay to reveal the white surface beneath (Pl. 11). The engine, or tool, was held by the lathe, and the technique could be used on curved surfaces. Josiah Wedgwood installed a lathe in 1763, after he had seen one in use at Matthew Boulton's factory at Soho, Birmingham, where it was employed in the manufacture of ornamental metalwork. Josiah's original machine is still in working order at the Barlaston factory. Many of the delicately tinted three-colour jasper wares have diced surfaces and these may be additionally ornamented with tiny coloured reliefs. Perhaps the most pleasing example of this form of decoration applied to vases appears on a lilac-coloured pair which are diced on part of the neck, the lower part of the body and part of the foot (Pl. 11). In the white areas where the tinted clay has been cut away are tiny green star-shaped *appliqués* (quatrefoils) which are repeated on the lid. Her Majesty Queen Mary, who was especially fond of pottery and porcelain, so admired these vases when she saw them displayed at the British Museum before 1914 that she had exact copies made.[78]

Figure 47 Blue jasper wine cooler (one of a pair) with polished interior, decorated with reliefs of Bacchanalian boys designed by Lady Diana Beauclerk, *c.* 1783, impressed WEDGWOOD. The same scene decorates the plaque on the clock in Fig. 91. H. 7¼ in (18.7 cm). Presented by Mr and Mrs Isaac Falcke, 1909.

Only a few of the pieces from the outstanding collection of jasper teawares, most of which were assembled by Mr and Mrs Isaac Falcke, can be mentioned and illustrated. Many are of such high quality that it is difficult to imagine them in use; perhaps they were intended from the start as cabinet pieces for display only. Some three-colour examples are illustrated on Pl. 11, including a blue dip straight-sided cup and saucer with highly elaborate reliefs consisting of goats' heads, swags and applied cameo medallions. A white jasper cup and saucer and a cream jug are amongst the masterpieces of the collection on account of the delicate colours of the ivy leaf and berry relief and the well-placed classical cameos. A tiny straight-sided custard cup with a finely formed twisted rope handle (Fig. 48) is a miracle of the potter's craft.

A sugar bowl and cover (Fig. 49) is ornamented with a relief of 'Domestic Employments' child groups by Emma Crewe. Miss Emma Crewe (fl. 1787–1818) was the daughter of a noted beauty, Mrs Crewe of Crewe Hall, Cheshire (see p. 68) who numbered amongst her friends Charles James Fox, Edmund Burke and Richard Brinsley Sheridan. It was no doubt through personal contact that her daughter began to supply designs to the potter. Between 1787 and 1818 she is thought to have produced designs for mother and child groups, and domestic employments (usually a small girl sewing or spinning) used on medallions, notably for jewellery, and often found on jasper teawares. The matching teapot and cover (Fig. 49) has a variant of the design by Lady Templetown in the 'Maternity' series, similar to that on p. 51. These series of designs by lady artists are all in much the same spirit, which has led to difficulties of attribution.

A few 'miscellaneous' pieces of jasper are notable for their period quality. One is a bell-pull with a small hole through the centre for a ribbon or rope (Pl. 11)

Figure 48 White jasper custard cup, lacking its lid, with blue dip on upper surface beneath a lattice of thin white jasper strips, impressed WEDGWOOD, *c.* 1780. H. 1¾ in (4.4 cm). Presented by Mr and Mrs Isaac Falcke, 1909.

which has applied white and yellow strapwork on a white jasper body, dipped blue and lathe-turned. Another, which was also presented by A. W. Franks,[79] is similar except that the strapwork is blue and green. The small oval white jasper medallion inscribed in blue BY/J.WEDGWOOD/F.R.S. has on the reverse 'N.º 7' in blue (Fig. 50). It was given to the Museum in 1907 by Charles Hercules Read, Keeper of British and Medieval Antiquities between 1896 and 1921, and was called a vase label 'used by Josiah Wedgwood in his showroom'. Harry Barnard, who had a long association with the firm, expressed the same opinion of its purpose[80] and as yet no new theory has been put forward. All this group of white jasper pieces are numbered in blue on the reverse, but the purpose of these numbers is not known. N.º 7 is the lowest of the series so far identified. The label may well have been made not long before Josiah's death in 1795 and after 1793. In this year the potter was elected a Fellow of the prestigious Royal Society in recognition of his work on an instrument for measuring heat which he called his thermometer and which he had demonstrated to the Society. Wedgwood is the only member of the Staffordshire potting fraternity ever to have been honoured in this way. He was also elected a Fellow of the Society of Antiquaries on 4 May 1786. This learned society was granted a Royal Charter by King George II in 1751, having come into organised existence half a century before [81] and it is a mark of Wedgwood's status that he was considered a suitable member of this august body.

One last category of jasper wares in the British Museum collection deserves our attention. Cameos and intaglios, some of three-colour jasper ware, were made in their hundreds for use in small items such as scent-bottles, earrings, snuff-box tops, *nécessaires* and other *objets de vertu*. Some are illustrated on Pl. 12. Amongst the historically interesting pieces is a white jasper ware medallion with a relief in

Figure 49 Part of a tea service: white jasper sugar bowl and cover decorated with pale blue dip partly removed by engine-turning to produce fluting, and ornamented with reliefs from the 'Domestic Employments' series designed by Lady Templetown, impressed WEDGWOOD (bowl), *c.* 1780. H. 4⅝ in (10.9 cm). Teapot and cover similarly decorated, ornamented with reliefs from the 'Maternity' series, impressed 'Wedgwood, o'. H. incl. knop 6 in (15.2 cm). Presented by Mr and Mrs Isaac Falcke, 1909.

black of a supplicating chained negro and the inscription 'Am I not a man and brother?'. It was modelled in 1787 after the seal for the Slave Emancipation Society like the caneware plaque shown in Pl. 13 and discussed on p. 45. Medallions were made to be worn in various ways, and there is another example of this subject in the collection mounted in gold.[82]

Wedgwood's interest in current affairs is also reflected in pieces produced at the time of the French Revolution. His correspondence during the summer of 1789 contains many references to this historic event, and as always he was quick to produce pieces for a changing market. Portraits made at this time are discussed on p. 84. A delightful small circular medallion in a metal mount (Pl. 12) has in relief emblems symbolic of the Revolution, a cornucopia, a bonnet of liberty on a stick and an olive branch contained within a fleur-de-lis border. The small charming and unusual jasper ware buckle (Pl. 12) with the relief inscription 'L'Amitie La Donne' ('The Gift of Friendship') was also made by Wedgwood presumably for the French market.

Earrings and beads (Pl. 12) are known from surviving pattern books to have been made at the factory. In a manuscript catalogue entitled 'Goods in the Catacombs taken an Account of Augt 27.th 1829',[83] that is, at the time of the sale of goods in the London showroom, there are drawings of earrings similar to those in the British Museum collection. Referred to as 'Jasper Whole Ear drops', there were 188 in stock. As a number of heads of George III, and 'Health Restor'd' medallions dating from 1789, were also in stock, there is no reason to rule out an eighteenth-century date of manufacture for the earrings. In the absence of factory marks and because of the prevalence of copying it is, however, possible that some pieces such as the earrings in the Falcke Collection might have been made by Josiah's Staffordshire rivals. As to classical subjects, three-colour jasper wares were made either in an oval or a circular format (Pl. 12) for use in box tops.[84] Some were mounted in cut steel, probably at Birmingham, and may have been used on belts, or inlaid into furniture. The uses for jasper ware were almost infinitely varied, and pieces such as the intaglio of a female sacrificing at an altar might have been used in a seal ring to seal a letter. So many aspects of eighteenth-century society, the wearing of patches, the taking of snuff, the sealing of letters, are brought more vividly to life by these tiny objects. The portrait medallions, which are the subject of the next chapter, provide an equally fascinating view of Josiah's contemporaries.

Figure 50 White jasper medallion decorated and inscribed in blue, thought to be a vase label. The inscription on the reverse, N.º 7, is the lowest number known on a piece of this type. After May 1793. L. 1⅞ in (4.8 cm). Presented by C. H. Read Esq., 1907.

3 Wedgwood and portraits

Jasper ware proved ideal for cameos imitating carved semi-precious stones and for portrait medallions. The growing influence of neoclassicism in the 1770s revived interest in the art of the gem-cutter, and as we have seen Wedgwood began by reproducing classical cameos and intaglios in black basalt. Portrait medallions were a particularly inspired idea because of the contemporary mania for collecting images of remarkable men and women past and present. In his first ever ornamental ware catalogue issued in 1773 of items 'sold at their rooms in Great Newport-Street, London', which included cameos, intaglios, medals and bas-reliefs, there were twenty different classes of pieces. Class X was entitled 'Heads of Illustrious Moderns, from CHAUCER to the present Time', whilst Class XI was 'Miscellaneous Heads, &c.' Class X is mentioned as being produced in black basalt as well as in 'polished Biscuit', almost certainly not jasper ware but an unglazed earthenware body. The vast majority of portraits Wedgwood produced show the sitter in profile in the manner of classical engraved gems. He was already poised to appeal to a vast market, as yet unsated with portraiture in wood, wax, paint, enamel and ivory, and was to produce an extensive range of portraits of his contemporaries in the 1770s and 80s. In a letter of 30 November 1776[1] to Paul Elers, son of Philip Elers (see p. 12), Wedgwood expressed some disappointment at the sales of his portraits of eminent men, but thought that in time the prejudice against pottery as a medium for portraiture might disappear. In any case he continued to expand his range of subjects and break into new markets. Many of these portraits probably ceased to be manufactured after Josiah's death, although some of the more popular specimens were reintroduced by the factory in the mid-nineteenth century when collecting Wedgwood jasper became fashionable.

Before the accession of the Falcke Gift in 1909 the portrait medallions were the most important part of the British Museum's Wedgwood collection and already numbered over 100 items.[2] Amongst the 522 items presented by Mr and Mrs Falcke (about 450 of which were Wedgwood) were between seventy and eighty portrait medallions in various ceramic materials. The collection as it now stands has been put together almost exclusively through the generosity of private collectors, who have always favoured medallions for their associations which they evoke. It represents extremely well the wide diversity of portrait medallions produced at the factory during the eighteenth century. An unusual nineteenth-century medallion is discussed in Chapter 7.

Wedgwood was by no means the first to make portrait medallions in ceramic material; they had been produced decades earlier at porcelain factories in Italy such as Doccia.[3] However, Josiah Wedgwood does appear to have been the first potter to make a large series of medallions which could be reproduced *ad infinitum* from moulds. His letters to Bentley provide valuable evidence of the sources used for the portraits, which were produced in a biscuit earthenware, black basalt, and

Plate 1 (*opposite*) Lead-glazed earthenware wall-vase, moulded with flowers, a fruiting vine and the head of Flora, 1754–9. H. 7 in (17.8 cm).

Plate 2a Creamware teapot and cover with surface decoration imitating agate and gilt ornamentation; Wedgwood and Bentley, *c.* 1771. H. 4¾ in (12 cm).

Plate 2b Creamware vases and covers on basalt plinths with surface decoration imitating agate and granite, gilt handles and ornaments; Wedgwood and Bentley, 1769–80. H. (*centre*) 6¾ in (17.1 cm); (*left and right*) 6¼ in (15.9 cm).

Plate 3 (*opposite*) Creamware plates transfer-printed in Liverpool with flower sprays and subjects from Aesop's *Fables*: (top) 'Hunted Beaver'; (*left*) 'Old Hound'; (*right*) 'Cock and the Fox'; (*bottom*) 'Lark and her Young Ones'. The ribbon and husk motif is painted, as is the rim, *c.* 1770–75. Diam. 9⅞ in (25 cm).

Plate 4 Creamware plate painted at the Chelsea workshop with a view of Mr Hopkins's Gardens, Painshill, Surrey, from the 'service with the green frog' made for the Empress Catherine the Great of Russia, 1773-4. Diam. 9¾ in (24.9 cm).

Plate 5 Creamware plate painted in enamel colours at the Chelsea workshop with 'Westcowes Castle, in the Isle of Wight', a so-called trial piece for the 'service with the green frog', 1773–4. Diam. $8\frac{7}{8}$ in (22.5 cm).

Plate 6a Black basalt plaque in metal frame painted in matt encaustic colours with a sacrifice scene from an engraving by Bartolozzi after Cipriani, probably decorated at the Chelsea workshop, *c.* 1775. L. without frame 13$\frac{11}{16}$ in (34.8 cm).

Plate 6b Black basalt (*from left to right*): vase painted with a cupid, *c.* 1775-95. H. 6$\frac{1}{2}$ in (16.5 cm); vase with snake handles, 1769-80. H. 13 in (33 cm); ewer with red encaustic painting, 1770-95. H. 10 in (25.3 cm); pair of vases painted with cupids, late 18th century. H. 6$\frac{1}{8}$ in (15.5 cm); cup and saucer with encaustic-painted trophies, *c.* 1785-1800. H. of cup 1$\frac{7}{8}$ in (4.8 cm). Diam. of saucer 5$\frac{1}{4}$ in (13 cm); *kantharos* flower vase, early 19th century. W. with handles 8$\frac{9}{16}$ in (21.7 cm); medallion with encaustic-painted scene of a charioteer, *c.* 1775-80. H. with frame 3$\frac{5}{8}$ in (8.4 cm); portrait medallion of W. Stukeley (1687-1765), *c.* 1775. H. 5$\frac{3}{4}$ in (14.5 cm).

Plate 7 (*opposite*) Jasper ware portrait plaque of Sir William Hamilton (1730-1803) in partly gilt wooden frame, 1779. H. with frame 15$\frac{3}{8}$ in (39.1 cm).

Plate 8 Pair of lustres with jasper ware drums with reliefs of Apollo (*left*) and another classical subject (*right*); the gilt-bronze perhaps made by Matthew Boulton at the Soho factory, Birmingham, the glass manufactured in London, *c.* 1790. H. 12¾ in (32.5 cm).

Plate 9 Black jasper ware copy of the Portland Vase, with 'nº 4' in pencil on the lip. The original is a cameo-glass vase of the 1st century AD in the British Museum. Wedgwood made between thirty to forty copies of the 'first edition' (it has been manufactured subsequently), *c.* 1790. H. 10 in (25.5 cm).

Plate 11 Coloured jasper ware, late 18th century (*from left to right*): coffee cup and saucer. H. of cup 2 9/16 in (6.5 cm). Diam. of saucer 4¾ in (12.1 cm); cream jug and cover. H. to top of knop 4⅛ in (10.4 cm); pair of vases with reliefs of Daedalus and Icarus and the 'sale of cupids'. H. 6⅛ in (15.5 cm); sugar bowl and cover. H. 5 in (12.6 cm); cup and saucer. H. of cup 2½ in (6.4 cm). Diam. of saucer 4¾ in (12.1 cm); saucer-dish. Diam. 4½ in (11.5 cm); bell-pull. H. 2¾ in (7 cm).

Plate 10 (*opposite*) Blue jasper ware vase and cover known as the Pegasus Vase from the figure of the flying horse on the cover. The scene represents the 'Apotheosis of Homer', or the crowning of a kitharist, copied from Hamilton's *Antiquities*. Presented to the British Museum by Josiah Wedgwood, 1786. H. 18 in (46 cm).

Plate 13 Caneware: vase and cover painted with a figure after Hamilton's *Antiquities*, 1780–95. H. to top of finial 7¾ in (19.5 cm); figure of Voltaire, 1779. H. 12¼ in (31.1 cm); medallion with kneeling slave in relief and basalt frame, modelled by Hackwood, 1787. H. 3¾ in (9.6 cm); teabowl and saucer, late 18th century. H. of bowl 1⅞ in (4.8 cm). Diam. of saucer 5⅛ in (13 cm).

Plate 12 (*opposite*) Jasper ware, late 18th century (*from top, left to right*): double-sided beads, probably Wedgwood. H. of each approx. ½ in (1.3 cm); button, Hercules carrying a boar. Diam. 1 in (2.5 cm); medallion in gilt-metal frame, Cupid on lion. Diam. 2⅛ in (5.3 cm); earrings, probably Wedgwood. L. 1½ in (3.8 cm); double-sided cameo, reliefs of figures symbolising Peace and War. Diam. 1 in (2.5 cm); button inscribed TALLY HO. Diam. 1¼ in (3.2 cm); medallion, Cupid as Oracle and zodiac border for a box top. Diam. 2⅝ in (6.6 cm); buckle inscribed L'AMITIE LA DONNE. L. 1⅜ in (3.5 cm); medallion in metal mount, cornucopia, bonnet of liberty, olive branch. Total H. 1¼ in (3.2 cm); Wedgwood and Bentley intaglio, sacrifice subject. H. 1 in (2.5 cm); ivory box mounted with medallion of Jove in border of pearls. L. of box 3¾ in (9.5 cm); smelling bottle, relief of Prince of Wales. H. 2⅝ in (6.6 cm); medallion, J. Necker (1732–1804) for box top. Diam. 2⅜ in (6 cm); circular medallion, sacrifice to Hygeia. Diam. 1¼ in (3.2 cm); three-colour plaque, sacrifice scene. L. 2 in (5.1 cm); medallion, Louis XVI. Diam. 2⅝ in (6.6 cm); oval medallion with cut steel mount, votaries of Diana. Total L. 4½ in (11.5 cm).

Plate 14a Pearlware plate printed in brown under the glaze, enamelled in orange and gilt with the 'Water Lily' pattern, 1806–11. Diam. 9¾ in (24.7 cm).

Plate 14b Lustred and gilt pearlware, *c.* 1810–15: shell comport. H. 9 in (22.9 cm); shell cream bowl, cover, stand and spoon. H. of bowl and cover 6⅛ in (15.5 cm); variegated lustre jug. H. 5¼ in (13.3 cm); ink-well. H. 3¼ in (7.9 cm); variegated lustre pecten-shell dish. L. 8¼ in (20.6 cm).

Plate 15a Caneware fish bowl decorated in enamel colours in the *famille rose* style, *c.* 1815. Diam. with handles 20 in (50.8 cm).

Plate 15b Creamware wall plaque painted with a girl in the Egyptian style. Signed by Thomas Allen, 1878. Diam. 15⅛ in (38.5 cm).

Plate 16 Earthenware vases designed by Keith Murray (1892–1981) with matt straw and matt green glaze by Norman Wilson, *c.* 1935. H. (*left*) 6½ in (16.5 cm); (*right*) 11¼ in (28.6 cm).

in jasper tinted various colours. Many of the earliest medallions, especially those in basalt with integral frames, appear to be directly based on medals. The process of manufacture was fairly complicated, and Josiah left no clear explanation of his method, so afraid was he of competitors obtaining his 'secrets'. When writing to Bentley of the constituents of his ceramic bodies he even used a code. However, he gives us in one letter, written on 1 and 2 August 1777 (E.25-18775), some idea of what was involved in producing a new 'head' from a medal, and explains to his partner why he perferred to work from a medal itself rather than from a mould of it:

> we . . . can take a clay mould from a medal, that will last for ever, & continue its sharp-ness, but from a mould we must first make a medal, then burn it & take a mould in clay from this burnt medal. This clay mould must likewise be burnt, & lastly the medals requir'd must be made out of these clay moulds, so that the operations are multiplied, & the medal diminish'd very much by our having our original in a mould, & not a medal.

The 'diminishing' he refers to is of course due to shrinkage in the firing. A letter of a few months earlier (E.25-18760) gives perhaps a clearer idea of the extent of 'diminishing' which could take place:

> In order to render our moulds everlasting, & allways sharp they should be made of *clay burnt*. For this purpose when we have a mould given to us, as in the case of the Muse, we are under the necessity of taking a press in clay out of the mould, & burning it. This is one diminishing of the size. – From this burnt impression we take a clay mould & burn that, which is a second lessening of the bassrelief, & from this mould we make the figures &c for sale which in our fine Jasper lessens the size very considerably.

A large number of old moulds of portrait medallions survive in the Wedgwood factory mould chamber. Numerous 'block moulds', as they are called, which are in relief and taken from the master mould, are preserved in the Wedgwood Museum at Barlaston. The working mould (again in intaglio), which was expend-able, was taken from the block mould. Medals were of course not the only models used; waxes and ivories, as well as portraits which had been engraved and plaster copies of portrait sculptures, were all reproduced in jasper ware. Wedgwood was aware that he had to utilise the work of craftsmen in other media, since no tradition of modelling in ceramic materials existed.

In the case of medallions modelled from life, or adapted from engravings or ivories, the usual first step was for the modeller, either Hackwood at the factory, or one of the sculptors specially employed by Wedgwood such as John Flaxman jun., John de Vaere or John Charles Lochée, to produce a wax from which a master mould was taken. Some of the fine original waxes have survived in both public and private collections, and there are examples in the British Museum which correspond to jasper medallions also in the collection (see p. 70).[4]

Some of the earliest portraits produced at Wedgwood take the form of plaques about 6 in (15 cm) high with suspension holes at the top and are of black basalt. An intregral part of the plaque is often a moulded frame of the same material. The reverse generally follows the contours of the portrait and therefore has an irregular surface, perhaps to prevent warpage in the firing. No marks are found on this type of plaque, but from the silky feel of the basalt the Museum's examples could well date from the early 1770s. The introduction to Class x in the Wedgwood and Bentley catalogue issued in 1773, the category containing 'Heads of Illustrious Moderns, from Chaucer to the present Time' states:

> Some of these Heads are made in the *black Basaltes*, and others in *polished Biscuit*, with *Cameo Grounds*; they are of various sizes and different Prices, from One Shilling a piece to a Guinea, with and without Frames of the same Composition; but most of them are from Two or Three Shillings to Seven Shillings and Sixpence each.

The plaque of the antiquarian William Stukeley (1687–1765) is a fine example of the basalt series (Pl. 6b). Stukeley's name is not mentioned in the list given in the

1773 Catalogue; it first occurs in the fourth edition produced in 1777. Wedgwood's portrait is directly based on a gold medal of Stukeley issued at the time of his death showing him aged fifty-four years according to its inscription.[5] The reverse of the medal shows a view of Stonehenge, referring to Stukeley's research on this and other antiquities which was published in 1740. The inscription gives the date of his death, and his age as eighty-four – a mistake, as he was in fact seventy-eight. Stukeley, a doctor of medicine, Fellow of the Royal Society and of the Society of Antiquaries, as well as Rector of the church in Queen's Square, not far from the site of the British Museum, where he is buried, was one of the greatest historian-antiquaries of his time. He was one of the earliest Trustees of the British Museum, being appointed in January 1753. Stukeley is depicted by the medallist in an idealised pose as a Roman emperor crowned with a laurel wreath, and Wedgwood clearly felt this representation was entirely suitable.

Another early portrait shows the Provençal-born philosopher, mathematician and astronomer, Pierre Gassendi (1592–1655). This basalt portrait (Fig. 51), which has a far less elaborate integral frame than the preceding example, is based on a medal by Warin of 1648.[6] Listed in the 1773 catalogue (in Class X), the subject

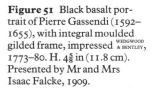

Figure 51 Black basalt portrait of Pierre Gassendi (1592–1655), with integral moulded gilded frame, impressed WEDGWOOD & BENTLEY, 1773–80. H. 4⅝ in (11.8 cm). Presented by Mr and Mrs Isaac Falcke, 1909.

Figure 52 Earthenware portrait of Plato (*c.* 429–347 BC), grey-blue dip, integral moulded frame painted black, polished relief, unmarked, *c.* 1770–80. H. 4¾ in (11.9 cm). Presented by Mr and Mrs Isaac Falcke, 1909.

was still in production in 1787 at the same price 'from one shilling a piece to a guinea, with and without frames of the same composition'. The average price of 2 or 3s to 7s 6d each mentioned in 1773 had dropped to 1s each by 1787, with the specification that these were in one colour and without frames. Some medallions of this format are difficult to date and were in production over a long period; however, the British Museum's Gassendi portrait bears the impressed mark of the partnership. No evidence has yet been found that the medallions of this type were originally gilded, and it may be that the rather dull gilding on this piece is of later date.

An earthenware medallion of Plato (Fig. 52) belongs to the category of Antique rather than Modern subjects. It is listed in Class III, 'Heads of Grecian Statesmen, Philosophers, Poets, &c', as number 27. The ground, incised with the philosopher's name, has been washed or dipped matt grey-blue, like the reverse, and the frame is painted black. The head itself is cream-coloured, and is covered with a glaze. It has a polished appearance and corresponds to the third composition listed in the introduction to the 1773 catalogue: 'A fine White Biscuit Ware, or *Terra Cotta*, polished and unpolished.' This kind of body does not appear in the augmented list, containing six bodies instead of three, given in the catalogue of 1787. Although doubts have been cast on the origin of this portrait, there is a mould for it in the Wedgwood factory mould chamber. Medallions of this type are uncommon, and were, it seems, made during the early period of the Wedgwood factory's existence.

A small medallion of the young Queen Charlotte (1744–1818) can be dated to the early 1770s (Fig. 53). It is made of white earthenware enamelled dark blue and washed lilac on the reverse. The potter used a medal as his source, copying the gold Coronation Medal by Louis Natter issued on 22 September 1761;[7] the same likeness can be seen on the medal commemorating the birth of the Prince of Wales in 1762. Wedgwood's career was somewhat bound up with the Queen, since he first fulfilled an order for her in 1765 and in 1767 called himself 'Potter to Her Majesty'.[8] She took considerable interest in the factory, visiting the showrooms in London on several occasions. Documents survive both at Windsor Castle and on loan to Keele University to demonstrate that a large quantity of Wedgwood earthenware was ordered and delivered to the Royal Family during the eighteenth century. There were several subsequent different editions in jasper ware of portraits of Queen Charlotte, each probably designed to form a pair with a medallion of King George III.[9]

Wedgwood was always conscious of the need to maintain a high standard of quality in order to sell his wares to the most elevated ranks of society at the best prices. His portrait medallions are amongst the most highly finished of all his productions, and he was lucky enough to be able to train up William Hackwood as a portrait modeller and finisher. Only two years after he had been taken on Hackwood was summoned at the express desire of a fashionable beauty of the day, Mrs Crewe, to model the head of her son. In a letter of 7 September 1771 (W/M 1441) Wedgwood writes to Bentley of having 'made a sort of beginning' with portraits, saying 'Hackwood has been three times at Crew by Mrs Crews particular desire to model the head of her son and heir. I told her he was quite a novice in Portrait modeling, but she wod have him try his hand & I could not refuse her. – What he will make of it I do not know'. In the event Hackwood proved to have talent as a modeller. A measure of the confidence he felt in his own powers as portrait modeller is his bold signature on the portrait of David Garrick (Fig. 54) taken from a medal of 1772 by Lewis Pingo, a cast of which was supplied by James Hoskins, a London plaster maker, in 1773. An account dated 16 January 1773 refers to two wax models from a sulphur (i.e. cast) of Mr Garrick at a cost of 8d.[10] Wedgwood did not approve of Hackwood's signing his work, as we learn from a letter he wrote to Bentley on 22 December 1777 (E.25-18805):

> I cannot resist the temptation of shewing [sic] my dear friend our new Shakespeare & Garrick though they are not so well fired as they should be, we put these into our common biscuit oven. You will see by looking under the shoulder of each that these heads are modeled [sic] by W[m]. Hackwood, but I shall prevent his exposing himself again now I have found it out. I am not certain that he will not be offended if he is refus'd the liberty of putting his name to the models which he makes quite new, & I shall be glad to have your opinion upon the subject. Mine is against any name being upon our articles besides W & B, & if you concur with me I will manage the matter with him as well as I can.

Hackwood was also responsible for modelling a portrait of Josiah himself (back cover). The basalt version in the British Museum collection bears the signature W.H on the truncation, hence there can be no doubt about its authorship. This portrait was almost certainly modelled from life and represents the potter as he must have appeared to his staff, rather than as the successful bewigged man of business depicted in an oil portrait in the Wedgwood Museum by Sir Joshua Reynolds executed in 1782, the same year as the Hackwood version.

Hackwood was by no means the only modeller employed by Wedgwood. As early as July 1774, when Wedgwood was still experimenting with the jasper body, Joachim Smith (c. 1737–1814), a well-known maker of portraits in wax who had

Figure 53 Biscuit earthenware portrait of the young Queen Charlotte (1744–1818), bevelled edge, ground enamelled mid-blue and washed pink on reverse. Unmarked. H. $\frac{3}{4}$ in (1.9 cm). Presented by A. W. Franks Esq.

Figure 54 Grey-blue jasper
portrait of David Garrick
(1717–79) with darker blue dip,
modelled by William Hack-
wood after a medal by Lewis
Pingo of 1772, in metal frame.
Impressed WEDGWOOD & BENTLEY, 1777–80.
H. to top of frame 4⅛ in
(10.5 cm). Presented by A. W.
Franks Esq.

completed a full-length wax model of the Prince of Wales for the King, was
working with Wedgwood. He may have asked Wedgwood to translate some of his
wax portrait heads into pottery. Smith's name first occurs in a letter of March
1774 when a forthcoming visit of Lady Charlotte Finch was mentioned.[11] An
extract from a letter of Wedgwood to Bentley written on 4 July 1774 (E.25-18544)
shows that the relationship between the potter and Smith was rather strained, for
Wedgwood was finding it difficult to cope with the new techniques of making
medallions.

> We find it necessary to make stamps for Mr Smiths Ladies heads, and by that means,
> with some fine bodies I have in hand I hope we shall do very cleverly. But those stamps
> require some time at first starting & I must beg of you to bespeak a little of Mr Smiths
> patience for us, & his Ladies shall be the better for it ever. Please to make my best compts
> to Mr Smith & tell him I do not forget him, but bear him in remembrance every day, and
> almost every hour & employ both my head & hands in his service continually.

The medallions were finished only shortly before 30 August, as another letter shows. Wedgwood wrote on that date (E.25-18555) that he was sending by coach 'a number of heads of Lady C[harlotte] F[inch's] Daughters'. One of the daughters of this governess of King George III's daughters was Henrietta Finch, two portraits of whom are in the British Museum collection. The earlier portrait, apparently of the waxen jasper composition, has an enamelled blue ground (Fig. 55), the other a lilac wash on the front only.[12] In the same letter Josiah continued to comment on the difficulties of working with 'these subtle' & complicated (though native) materials' which he was using for the new (jasper ware) body. He complained that he needed 'more *time*, more *hands*, & more *heads*' and wished that he had nothing else to do but his experiment work, concluding the letter plaintively: 'Farewell – I am almost crazy.'

On 12 December 1774 (E.25-18573) Josiah wrote to his partner:

> I thought you would lose Mr. Smith, but we must not lose the business if it be possible to keep it, as we can now certainly make the finest things in the world for Portraits. – Pray try to obtain another modeler [*sic*] if Mr. Smith is gone, & a polisher, or rather a shop of Polishers will be *absolutely necessary*, & the sooner the better.

The polishers were required to finish the edges of the medallions, many of which were bevelled and worked on the lapidary wheel.

Josiah's dealings with Joachim Smith were not a success. Smith's name rarely appears in Wedgwood's letters to Bentley after early 1775, when the sculptor apologised for not having sent anything for months because of numerous accidents to moulds and even to models.[13] However, the potter was not deterred from looking for other modellers: in September 1774 he wrote to Bentley (E.25-18558):

> I am glad you have given Lochee something to do. We want a great deal of modeling [*sic*], having many things before us within a little of being capital. The small Bass relief Heads of Eminent Men, Greeks &c should be made more complete, & extensive. If Lochee is capable of anything in that stile you may venture to engage him for a time. We could employ him here for a year or two repairing Busts [that is, putting together the separate parts of a moulded piece] & Figures if we durst have him in the country for Hackwood is of the greatest value and consequence in finishing fine small work, and of this kind we have and shall have enough to employ him in constantly.

John Charles Lochée, who was born in 1751, became a famous sculptor and portrait modeller in wax,[14] but in 1774 he was still unknown. In September of the same year, as we have seen, Wedgwood was even considering employing him at the factory itself, at the risk of offending Hackwood. Lochée exhibited at the Royal Academy for the first time in 1776, giving his address as 17 King Street, Soho. Wedgwood still had dealings with him some thirteen years later: in December 1787 he was in Wedgwood's employment and was copying gems in the collection of the Marquess of Buckingham at Stowe, a task which was in progress at least until March the following year.[15] A letter dated 24 March 1788 (W/M 1460) from Josiah Wedgwood II to his father shows that business connections with Lochée had not been severed, although Lochée's work was not entirely satisfactory:

> Now you are in London it would be very kind if you would give Mr Lochee a lecture on modelling & making [plaster] moulds – you know how he undercuts – & his moulds are in general very bad, sometimes they appear to have had waxes taken out of them – & I believe always they are very full of pin holes.

These comments are quite surprising set against the pretensions of the modeller who by 1786 was calling himself on his trade card 'Portrait Modeller to Prince William Henry'. By 1786 he had become a specialist in portraiture in wax and had moved from Soho to 11 Rupert Street, Haymarket. Lochée's waxes, examples of which are in the British Museum collection, were used as models for portraits of various members of the Royal Family.[16] A wax of Prince Edward, Duke of Kent

Figure 55 'Waxen jasper' medallion of Henrietta Finch (dates unknown) enamelled in blue, the reverse purplish-grey, unmarked, *c*. 1773. H. to top of frame 1¾ in (4.5 cm). Presented by A. W. Franks Esq.

Figure 56 Blue jasper portrait of Prince Edward Augustus, Duke of Kent (1767–1820), fourth son of George III, modelled by John Charles Lochée, *c.* 1787, in metal frame, impressed WEDGWOOD. H. incl. frame 3½ in (9 cm). Presented by A. W. Franks Esq.

(1767–1820), fourth son of King George III, was clearly the model for Wedgwood's jasper portrait (Fig. 56).[17] A payment to Lochée for 'Models of the Royal Princes' dated 8 May 1787 and recorded on a receipt of 5 August 1790 in the Royal Archive at Windsor Castle[18] may refer to the production of the wax, and it is likely that the jasper version was produced at around the same time. The general proportions of the bust within its frame have been faithfully preserved in the ceramic version. In this instance, as in others, it is striking to note how closely the potter followed his source, merely translating it into a different medium.

Another wax modeller who was useful to Wedgwood was John de Vaere (1755–1830). Of French origin, he attended the Royal Academy Schools in 1786 and was recommended to Wedgwood by John Flaxman. Until 1790 he worked with Flaxman and Henry Webber in Rome (see p. 118) and succeeded Webber

Figure 57 Green jasper dip portrait of Sir John Jervis, first Earl of St Vincent (1735–1823), modelled by John de Vaere, 1798, in metal frame, impressed WEDGWOOD. H. to top of frame 4¼ in (10.9 cm). Presented by Mr and Mrs Isaac Falcke, 1909.

himself as chief modeller in the ornamental department in 1794. He had the distinction of modelling a set of four portraits of the great naval heroes, Admirals Nelson, Duncan, Howe and St Vincent in 1798, and his fine red waxes survive in the Wedgwood Museum, although they are now in a fragmentary state after being damaged by flood.[19] The British Museum collection contains jasper ware portraits of Nelson,[20] Howe[21] and the Earl of St Vincent (Fig. 57). Sir John Jervis, First Earl of St Vincent (1735–1823), was put in command of the Mediterranean fleet in 1797 and defeated the Spanish off Cape St Vincent. The medallion was issued not long after this victory for which he received an earldom and a pension. After subduing unrest amongst British sailors, he introduced a number of reforms as First Lord of the Admiralty between 1801 and 1804. The jasper portrait reveals a straightforward resolute character, perhaps somewhat idealised like the other portraits in the same series and like them all characterised by a severe profile pose. The cracking of the surface of the portrait is an unusual

Figure 58 Blue jasper portrait of General Sir Eyre Coote (1726–83), modelled by Eley George Mountstephen, 1788, in metal frame, impressed WEDGWOOD. H. to top of frame 5¼ in (13.3 cm).

feature due perhaps to a faulty mixing of a particular batch of the jasper body; the white relief is, however, crisply finished and suggests a date of manufacture in the late eighteenth century.

A fine example of the work of Eley George Mountstephen (active 1781–91), a sculptor of Irish origin whose short life has not yet been fully studied, is the portrait of General Sir Eyre Coote (1726–83, Fig. 58). After fighting in the '45 against the Young Pretender, Prince Charles Edward Stuart, Coote made his career in India where he became Commander-in-Chief in 1777. The subject of the medallion was for many years wrongly identified as Ferdinand IV, King of the Two Sicilies, but is now known to represent Coote. Mountstephen modelled the portrait at the end of June, or beginning of July 1788, possibly specially for Lady Coote.[22] He appears to have used a bust of 1779 by Joseph Nollekens as his source.[23] The Wedgwood portrait medallion is in extremely high relief and presents an unusual full-face view. Mountstephen is recorded at four different London

Figure 59 Grey-blue jasper portrait of Dr Daniel Charles Solander (1736–1782), modelled in 1775, in metal frame, impressed Wedgwood & Bentley. H. to top of frame 3⅝ in (9.2 cm). Presented by Mr and Mrs Isaac Falcke, 1909.

addresses, but the correspondence with Wedgwood's nephew, Byerley, who managed the London showrooms after Bentley's death, on the subject of this portrait is written from Buckinghamshire.[24]

The greatest artist who worked for Wedgwood was undoubtedly John Flaxman and his career in relationship to the Wedgwood firm is discussed in Chapters 2 and 5. His contribution to Wedgwood's production of portrait medallions was also an important one. A portrait which has particular significance in the context of the history of the Museum is that of Dr Daniel Charles Solander (1736–82), the Swedish naturalist and pupil of Linnaeus who was employed at the Museum as assistant librarian from 1763 (Fig. 59). He was closely connected with Sir Joseph Banks with whom he travelled on Cook's first voyage in the *Endeavour* (1768–71) to observe the transit of Venus. The portrait of Solander was modelled as a

Figure 60 Grey-blue jasper portrait of Captain James Cook (1728–1779), dark blue dip, bevelled edge with blue dip line, modelled by John Flaxman jun., 1779, in metal frame, impressed Wedgwood & Bentley. H. to top of frame 3¾ in (9.6 cm). Presented by A. W. Franks Esq.

companion to an early version of Banks,[25] and both are referred to in a letter from Wedgwood to Bentley of 25 July 1775 (E.25-18617): 'I wish you to see Mr Flaxman before you leave London, & if you could prevail upon him to finish Mr Banks & Dr Solander they would be an acquisition to us.' The botanist, who was secretary and librarian at Banks's house in Soho Square from 1771, was himself useful to the partnership in their quest for new subjects, as is evident in a letter dated 8 May 1779 (E.26-18889) to Bentley from his partner: 'Pray . . . inquire for some *notorious heads* of foreigners, either in busts, – Medallians [*sic*] or prints. The Museum is a likely place, & Dr Solander your man.'

Two remarkable portraits of Captain James Cook (1729–79) were produced by Wedgwood, and both are represented in the British Museum collection. The earlier portrait (Fig. 60) is an unusual three-quarter full-face view which was in

Figure 61 Pale blue jasper portrait of Captain James Cook (1728–1779), modelled by John Flaxman jun., *c.* 1784, in metal frame, impressed WEDGWOOD. H. to top of frame 4⅛ in (10.6 cm). Presented by A. W. Franks Esq.

production by 21 August 1779 when it appears in the factory's 'Oven Book', or record of firings. It is traditionally attributed to John Flaxman and is after a portrait by William Hodges, an artist who travelled with Cook on his voyage of 1772–5. The present location of the painting is unknown; but it was engraved in 1777 by James Basire as a frontispiece to *A Voyage towards the South Pole and Round the World*. The Wedgwood portrait was listed in the firm's catalogue of 1779. The later portrait shows Cook in profile (Fig. 61). It was probably adapted from a medal by Lewis Pingo struck in 1779 for the Royal Society.[26] An unsigned wax of this portrait attributed to Flaxman is in a private collection.[27] A bill dated 24 January 1784 (E.2-1339) records that Wedgwood paid Flaxman two guineas for 'A Model in wax of Capt:^{n} Cook' but it is not known for certain to which of the two Cook portraits this wax refers.

The profile portrait is far more formal and severe than the earlier version. The latter is a more pleasing work as the shape of the relief is well-proportioned to its ground and it has been produced with an especially refined edge. The earlier plaque is formed of solid grey jasper, the surface of the medallion surrounding the relief head has been washed mid-blue, with a dark blue line painted around the centre of the edge so that the grey area nearest the ground of the portrait has the effect of setting off the head of the sitter. This decorative effect, which can be detected in the illustration, seems to be restricted to medallions produced during the Wedgwood and Bentley partnership.

A further example of Flaxman's portrait modelling for Wedgwood has several unusual features. The production of this full-face portrait on a black ground of Maria I, Queen of Portugal (1734–1816, Fig. 62), is documented in a bill for the sculptor's work dated 1 June 1787 (E.2-1339), 'A model of the Queen of Portugal . . . £3 3'. Flaxman's wax portrait was sent to Etruria in June and was in produc-

Figure 62 Black jasper dip portrait of Queen Maria I of Portugal (1734–1816), modelled by John Flaxman jun., 1787, after a porcelain cameo by João de Figueireido, 1782, for the Lisbon Porcelain Factory, impressed WEDGWOOD. H. 4 in (10 cm). Presented by Joseph Mayer Esq., FSA, 1853.

Figure 63 Grey-blue jasper ware portrait of Christ, impressed WEDGWOOD & BENTLEY, 1774–80. H. 3 in (7.5 cm). Presented by F. Howard Paget Esq., 1937.

tion before the end of the year. He probably used as his source a porcelain cameo made at the Lisbon Porcelain Manufactory. An example of this diminutive cameo set in a silver-gilt finger ring is in the British Museum collection; it is signed by João Figueireido and dated 1782.[28] The jasper version was presumably produced by Wedgwood as part of an attempt to capture the export market.

Another unusual and rare jasper medallion undoubtedly made for the overseas market depicts the head of Christ (Fig. 63) wearing a type of halo often found in medallic representations of Our Lord. No source has yet been discovered and no other example from the Wedgwood and Bentley period has been published. A letter from Wedgwood to Bentley of 5 November 1774 (E.25-18561) on the subject of a cargo for Cadiz *en route* for Mexico casts some light on the kind of articles he was prepared to make, and may help to date the British Museum medallion:

I apprehend some articles shod be made on purpose for this trade relative to their Religion. They will wear Crucifixes, Saints &c for Bracelets, Lockets, Snuffboxes &

other matters. In one of the orders we were told not to send anything more than was order'd, unless we had any Saints of which we might send some.

It seems highly likely that the reason so few of these medallions are known is that they were originally sent to non-English speaking countries where Wedgwood collecting has never become a serious passion.

Perhaps the most remarkable of all the portraits made by Wedgwood are those completed not long before Thomas Bentley's death. They measure no less than 10 in (25.4 cm) in height. Although they were something of a technical achievement, there is no mention in surviving letters of production problems. The series included outstanding scientists and others – Sir William Hamilton, whose influence on British cultural life at this time was considerable; Sir Joseph Banks, himself a naturalist and President of the Royal Society for over four decades; and the American statesman Benjamin Franklin. All are shown in suitably noble style. Sir William Hamilton (1730–1803) was, both directly and indirectly, one of the potter's chief mentors. Portraits of him had been produced as early as 1772 from a model supplied by Joachim Smith,[29] and examples of these earlier, more realistic, versions of the sitter are in the British Museum collection.[30] The highly idealised but strongly modelled portrait (Pl. 7) produced in 1779 shows him without his full wig, elegant coat and Order of the Bath, which he received in 1772. A letter of 9 May 1779 (E.25-18890) from Wedgwood to his partner reveals that the potter had some misgivings about the quality of the jasper portrait: 'S[r] W (illia) [m] H (amilton) [s] Head is too large even for his big body – When that was diminish'd it became a monster.' However, the portrait went into production and in another letter, written on 2 September 1779 (E.26-18920), Wedgwood asked Bentley if he could think of a better partner than Count Caylus, as a 'match' or companion for 'our very good friend S[r] Wm Hamilton'. Caylus's *Receuil d'Antiquités* was published in five volumes between 1752 and 1788, influencing Wedgwood's choice of decorative motifs through its large collection of engravings of classical antiquities. In the same letter Wedgwood continued: 'We have bosted [*sic*] him out (S[r] W[m]) the size of Mr. Banks, & I think a suit of eminent moderns, naturalists, amateurs &c should be made of the same size, & stile, & so form a constellation, as it were, to attract the notice of the great, & illuminate every palace in Europe.'

The portrait of Banks (1743–1820, illustrated in Fig. 64) is again a subsequent version, the earlier one having been modelled by John Flaxman jun. in 1775.[31] Banks was made a baronet in 1781 and became a member of the Order of the Bath in 1795. Wedgwood's name appears in a diary kept by Banks[32] in December 1767, and on 17 September 1771 Wedgwood wrote to Bentley in terms which reveal the connection between this cultivated man and the highest circles of taste and learning.[33]

I rejoyce, & enjoy with you all your good doings with your good Lord Hope, your Banks's & your Solanders & thank you very sincerely for the rich entertainment you have lately feasted me with & must beg leave to take these late things you have by this time enjoy'd with as particular an account of them as your time will permit.

Flaxman is likely to have been responsible for the Banks portrait plaque, a fine neoclassical work of 1779, since there is a bill from him (L.1-206) for 'the Portrait of Mr. Banks modelled in Clay . . .£2 2s' dated 21 August 1779. It has been suggested that behind Flaxman's plaque lies an unrecorded portrait relief by the sculptor Giuseppe Cerrachi (1751–1801).[34] Banks is shown without wig, and the drapery pinned at his left shoulder is distinctly reminiscent of a toga. In a letter to Bentley of 2 September 1779 (E.26-18920) Wedgwood recorded his progress with several medallions and commented on the distinctly severe appearance of this particular sitter: 'We have finish'd the Herborisieur [Lin-

naeus], & are now modeling [*sic*] a head of Dᵣ Solander to match Mr. Banks, the second, & large edition, which I think a good head, & a very strong likeness, but the original does not seem to have sat in an over pleasant mood.'

In later life Banks's despotism in regard to the Royal Society was well-known, and may have been a direct result of the gout from which he suffered for a long period. He is seen in this portrait as a mature man, the veteran of a voyage to Labrador and Newfoundland in his twenties, with Captain Cook in the *Endeavour* between 1768 and 1771 and of an expedition to Iceland in 1772. In the previous year he had been elected President of the Royal Society of which he had been a Fellow since 1766. By virtue of his appointment he became *ex officio* a Trustee of the British Museum and remained actively involved with the Museum until the end of his life, being one of its great benefactors.

A much earlier President of the Royal Society (1703–27) was the mathematician Sir Isaac Newton (1642–1727) whose portrait was in production at Wedgwood at the time of the catalogue issued in 1773. The large version in the British Museum collection (Fig. 65) shows a three-quarters full-face view with a comet at the right. The comet presumably refers to that part of Newton's *Principia*, in which he demonstrated the theory of gravity, relating to the theory of comets. This section was the cause of some controversy between Hooke and Halley who assisted Newton with his publication, and was the last part to be completed. Work was in progress on the portrait in spring 1779 according to a letter written by Wedgwood on 24 March,[35] and the plaque was intended to be a companion to a portrait of another great scientist, Dr Joseph Priestley (1733–1804). Firing of this version took place on 10 April when it is mentioned in the 'Oven Book'.[36]

There is yet another large jasper portrait plaque (Fig. 66) from the same series depicting the American statesman Benjamin Franklin (1706–90). Franklin too was immensely interested in science, carrying out experiments to determine the cause of lightning and investigating electricity. His role in the War of American Independence fascinated Wedgwood and his partner who closely followed the events of 1776. The first portrait in a series of no fewer than eight different versions of Franklin is thought to have been created in about 1775,[37] the rest following within a few years. The large version corresponds with an unusual small medallion in the British Museum collection[38] and is also an idealised portrait without wig. Thomas Bentley was a co-founder with Franklin of a club of thirteen meeting at Old Slaughter's Coffee House in St Martin's Lane 'for the discussion of a philosophical ritual'. Wedgwood also became a member of the club which was in existence from as early as 1773.[39]

The large plaques were intended almost as substitutes for paintings. At the other end of the spectrum were portraits which were designed to be incorporated into *objets de vertu*, such as snuffboxes. By 2 July 1776 Wedgwood was ready to manufacture these, as is evident in a letter to his partner (E.25-18679):

> For inlaying in Snuff boxes our Kings & Queens will be very good things *for England*. We can make other Kings & Queens, & eminent Heads for other Countries & such subjects will be the most likely to go in quantities, for People will give more for *their own Heads*, or the *Heads in Fashion*, than for any other subjects, & buy abundantly more of them . . .

Heads were also applied to scent flasks and 'smelling bottles', as Josiah called them. Examples of both these groups can be found in the British Museum. A bust of King George IV as Prince of Wales in white jasper ornaments a smelling bottle (Pl. 12) of blue jasper. On the reverse are the Prince of Wales's feathers and his motto ICH DIEN. The portrait is a rather unpretentious one as the Prince is shown without the Order of the Garter. The major part of this charming object is made of two circular discs of clay joined by means of a central strip concealed by white jasper laurel leaf and berry ornament. It fits comfortably in the hand and is

Figure 64 Blue jasper portrait of Joseph Banks (1743–1820), modelled by John Flaxman jun., 1779, in metal frame, impressed WEDGWOOD & BENTLEY. H. of plaque 10¼ in (26 cm). Presented by A. W. Franks Esq.

Figure 65 Grey-blue jasper portrait of Sir Isaac Newton (1642–1727) with blue dip, perhaps modelled after an ivory carving by Silvanus Bevan, in metal frame, impressed ^{WEDGWOOD} _{& BENTLEY}, 1779–80. H. to top of frame 11½ in (29.1 cm). Presented by A. W. Franks Esq.

Figure 66 Grey-blue jasper portrait of Benjamin Franklin (1706–1790) with blue dip, in metal frame, impressed WEDGWOOD & BENTLEY, 1779–80. Franklin is shown in Roman dress, whereas on a number of other Wedgwood portraits he is depicted in contemporary costume and is far more lifelike. H. incl. frame 11½ in (29.2 cm). Presented by A. W. Franks Esq.

modelled in low relief for practical reasons. On either side the edge and the central part enclosing the relief have been finely turned, defining a border filled by wreaths and ovals containing flowers. It is likely to have been made in spring 1788, for Wedgwood's letters at this period contain references to other smelling bottles ornamented with reliefs.

The same meticulous attention to finish has been paid to two snuffbox tops of dark blue jasper dip. A similar effect achieved by turning has been attained on a portrait of the French banker and statesman Jacques Necker (1732–1804) enclosed by a decorative border containing fleurs-de-lis (Pl. 12). The portrait, related to an anonymous medal,[40] is a three-quarters full-face view well proportioned to the area it occupies. The edge has been bevelled and polished on the lapidary wheel. These medallions were in production at a time when Necker was playing a vital role in French affairs after attempting fiscal reforms when appointed Director-General of Finance in 1777 and recommending in 1788 that the Estates General be summoned. The following year in July (W/M 1460) Josiah Wedgwood II reported to his father 'We are making Mr Neckers head of a size proper for snuff box tops'. In the same series is a portrait of Louis XVI of France (1754–1793), also medallic in style (Pl. 12). On this piece the border ornament in relief is not enclosed and consists of fleurs-de-lis alternating with ovals.

The crisply modelled and sometimes highly lifelike portraits, such as that of Henrietta Finch, preserve a lasting appeal. Jasper portrait medallions have enjoyed a long period of popularity with collectors and the general public alike. As a mirror of their age the portraits of scientists, antiquarians, military and naval heroes and other public figures reflect with remarkable fidelity the preoccupations of the educated class in eighteenth-century Britain.

BUSTS

In the first ornamental catalogue of 1773 under Class XII twenty-three 'busts, small statues, boys, animals &c.' were listed. The British Museum's collection does not include any pieces from this list which bear the impressed mark of the partnership. The production of basalt library busts was being stepped up in the following year: many were closely based on plaster models supplied by the leading London plaster shops, which were occasionally under the direction of sculptors of some talent, such as Henry Cheere (1709–87), who had premises at Hyde Park Corner.[41] A letter to Bentley of 11 September 1774 (E.25-18558) gives some idea of work in progress on the new range of sculpture:

> I must send you a few of the new model'd figures as they are, for Hackwood, if he is capable of giving character to their faces, & improving the draperies, w[ch]. I have some doubt of, though I am perswaded [sic] he would mend them considerably, he has no time for it at present. – The Busts will employ him for a year or two before our collection is tolerably complete, & I am much set upon having it so, being fully perswaded [sic] they will be a capital article with us, & Hackwood finishes them admirably – They are infinitely superior to the Plaister [sic] ones we take them from, as you will see more fully when you came to Etruria. I hope in time to send you a collection of the *finest Heads* in this World.

Casts for a bust of the Roman emperor Marcus Aurelius (AD 121–80) were supplied to Etruria in 1774 by the plaster makers James Hoskins and Benjamin Grant of London at a cost of one and a half guineas. Its exact source is unknown but it may have been adapted from a marble in the Capitoline Museum, Rome.[42] A fine example (Fig. 67) exists in the British Museum collection. Although it is polished, the author sees no trace of the 'bronze' finish, recorded when it came into the Museum in 1909. A bust of the poet Geoffrey Chaucer (?1340–1400), the

101.
MARCUS AURELIUS
BASALT WARE, BRONZED. ABOUT 1780.
Falcke Coll. 1909.

Figure 67 Black basalt bust of
Marcus Aurelius (AD 121–80),
impressed ^{Wedgwood}_{& Bentley}, 1774–80.
H. incl. circular stand 15½ in
(39.5 cm). Presented by Mr and
Mrs Isaac Falcke, 1909.

model for which was supplied by Hoskins and Grant in 1775,[43] with a circular plinth decorated with a Greek key motif (Fig. 68) has always been considered to date from the Wedgwood and Bentley period even though it is unmarked. Similar bases are found on marked examples, and the basalt is of fine quality.

A diminutive portrait marble by another French eighteenth-century sculptor, Jean-Claude Rosset, called Du Pont (1703 or 1706–86), measuring $13\frac{3}{4}$ in (35 cm) and dated 1773[44] was the basis of a most unusual small-scale figure of the *philosophe* Voltaire (1694–1778) produced in the caneware composition during the Wedgwood and Bentley period (Pl. 13). Basalt versions of this piece are much more common, the cane-coloured version having the additional merit of being mentioned in a letter from Wedgwood to Bentley. It may be remembered that the potter was still experiencing problems in producing cane-coloured ware in July or September 1779 (see p. 45). On 16 October (E.26-18931) he wrote to his partner:

> We send you two small statues of Voltaire and Rousseau made of cane color clay, but you will find them both so much discolour'd in burning as to stand in need of a wash of paint. We cover'd them close in burning, knowing how apt this body is to turn brown but in vain . . . I hope to overcome this evil, but it must be in a new body the present is incorrigible.

The British Museum figure is slightly discoloured, but this appears to be the result of the passage of time rather than of problems encountered in firing.[45] The crispness of the modelling shows what standard of excellence the firm could achieve in this kind of work.

Wedgwood's portrayal of both classical and contemporary figures embraced a uniquely broad range of subjects in systematic fashion. Although other pottery and porcelain factories in England and on the Continent produced both busts and medallions, none manufactured them in comparable quantities or for such a long period of time as Wedgwood. As we shall see, the art of portraiture continued to appeal to the public, if only on a limited scale in the nineteenth century following the death of the firm's founder.

Figure 68 Black basalt bust of the poet Chaucer (1340–1400), attached to cylindrical support which rests on the circular plinth, unmarked, probably *c.* 1775–80. H. $14\frac{1}{8}$ in (36 cm). Presented by A. W. Franks Esq.

4 Painting on eighteenth-century Wedgwood

Examples of painting on creamware, basalt, pearlware and caneware can be found in the British Museum collection. An enamelled caneware fish bowl made in the early part of the nineteenth century (Pl. 15a) is discussed in Chapter 7. Josiah even congratulates Bentley in a letter[1] on his success in enamelling in jasper ware. This technique seems to have been tried experimentally about 1775, and the potter thought that he might make enamelled cameos and intaglios for bracelets and rings.

The technique of enamelling on pottery consists in the simplest terms of painting freehand over the glaze with a glassy substance, in other words enamel, coloured with metal oxides. It is the final process to be carried out on pieces which have been glazed. Although a far lower temperature than that required for the biscuit firing of creamware will fuse the glassy substances to any ceramic body, different pigments require different temperatures to reach their maturing point. This means that it is sometimes necessary to fire one piece several times at the decorating stage. Painting in the encaustic technique on basalt and other unglazed pieces is more durable than overglaze painting on earthenwares. This technique is a decorative process always firmly associated with Josiah Wedgwood, since he patented it in November 1769, and it is one about which we know a certain amount. It involves painting on black basalt or cane-coloured ware in matt colours usually to simulate Greek red-figured vases. In the 1773 catalogue issued by Wedgwood and Bentley under Class XIX is a discursive note on the history and nature of this technique. The 'Etruscan Colours', as the catalogue calls them, are '*burnt in, smooth* and *durable* but without *any glassy lustre*'. Although the exact formula has never been published,[2] it is clear that the usual fluxing agent producing a shiny surface was omitted from the composition. The process was especially well suited to the manufacture of vases closely based on Greek originals, which became immensely popular in fashionable circles in the early 1770s.

Much hand-painting on Wedgwood pieces was done outside the factory premises at Burslem and Etruria. By around the middle of the eighteenth century it had become the practice, as we have seen, to sub-contract many aspects of pottery manufacture including decoration. In the case of Wedgwood's useful wares made at Burslem it is known that David Rhodes of Leeds and his partner Jasper Robinson were responsible for their decoration from around 1763–4. The painting on a creamware teapot with lively but somewhat crudely executed stylised flowers (Fig. 69) is generally attributed to David Rhodes and Company about 1770. However, since Rhodes was more concerned at that date with decorating ornamental pieces, the teapot may perhaps date from several years earlier. Despite the persistence of the rococo style exemplified in the decoration of the teapot and in its form, it is hard to imagine that a purely utilitarian piece painted in such an unsophisticated manner was a product of the London enamelling work-

Figure 69 Creamware teapot with cabbage-moulded handle and spout, unmarked, but attributed to Josiah Wedgwood on the grounds of its shape; painted in overglaze colours in the Leeds workshop of David Rhodes and Jasper Robinson, probably *c.* 1763/4–68. H. incl. lid $6\frac{1}{8}$ in (15.5 cm). Bequeathed by Miss C. M. Woodward, 1981.

shop. It appears that Rhodes moved to the capital in 1768, where he worked for Wedgwood in rooms in St Martin's Lane, Covent Garden. In the following year Wedgwood tried hard to persuade Bentley to send Rhodes to Burslem, as is evident from the potter's letters to his partner,[3] but Rhodes was still in London in January 1770 working for the ornamental partnership and as far as we know never moved to Staffordshire. He was the main enameller for Wedgwood and Bentley in London until his death in 1777 and from September 1769 was entrusted with the decoration of black Etruscan vases.

Despite the fact that Rhodes was taking creamware for decoration from Wedgwood's useful partnership, there was still work for other painters. John Sadler and Guy Green are mainly associated with transfer-printing, in which they specialised, and their work for Wedgwood has already been mentioned (see p. 16). However, this Liverpool partnership also arranged for the painting of the green husks around the transfer print as well as the edges of plates in the Fable series (Pl. 3). The small purple flowers scattered on the rim of the plate printed with the scene known as the 'Corinthian Ruins' (Fig. 9) were also doubtless painted in the workshops of Sadler and Green or through their agency. Some subjects, such as the shell series (Fig. 10), were printed and then washed over with colour. However, scholars have not yet discovered from the surviving correspondence between Sadler and Green and Josiah Wedgwood loaned to Keele University the details of the organisation of painting in what was essentially a printing establishment. As several of the Liverpool porcelain factories were also using Sadler and Green to print their wares, it is probable that the painting on Wedgwood's creamwares was done by one of the numerous porcelain painters in the locality.

In the late 1760s Josiah Wedgwood and Thomas Bentley seem to have been employing several painters to decorate pieces at Burslem. The name of James Bakewell occurs more than once in Josiah's correspondence with Thomas Bentley, and his initials are found on a number of creamwares of deep cream colour. These are generally painted in puce with carefully delineated naturalistic

Figure 70 Creamware plate with moulded edge painted in overglaze puce with a narcissus and a star-shaped flower, unmarked, painting attributed to James Bakewell, *c.* 1768–70. Diam. $8\frac{1}{2}$ in (21.6 cm). Presented by Mr and Mrs Isaac Falcke, 1909.

flowers: the plate illustrated in Fig. 70 can be attributed to Bakewell, or perhaps to one of the painters or paintresses working with him. The names of two of these, Catherine Dent and Thomas Green, appear in an account for enamelling dated October 1770.[4]

The considerable expansion of both the useful and ornamental businesses at the close of the 1760s made Josiah decide to take on more painters. He became rather anxious about hiring them. A letter of 25 February 1768[5] to Bentley shows that he was thinking about setting up a painting workshop but was not yet ready to do so. In the summer of that year he was taking on painters for Etruria who had already been trained and had worked at porcelain factories. This was certainly easier than attempting to school them from scratch. Wedgwood seems to have found painters, who considered themselves of superior status, extremely difficult to deal with, and he sounds particularly exasperated in a letter to Bentley written in September 1769 (E.25-18254):

> I wrote to you concerning Warburton a Painter, but have since learn't that he will do us no good he is so poor a hand even at common India patt[ns]. All these matters I leave to yours & Mr. Crofts better management. I have enough to do to make the Potts, & manage the Pottmakers though I wo[d]. rather, man for man, have do with a shop of Potters than Painters.

The 'Mr Crofts' mentioned here may be the copper enameller William Hopkins Craft (?1730–1810), a partner of the pottery enameller David Rhodes for two years between 1768 and 1770.

In 1769 and 1770 Josiah's chief concern was to make, decorate and sell as many encaustic vases as possible in the short time before his competitors began to copy them. Almost as soon as he had taken out his patent for the encaustic process he realised that it could not remain secret for long. He wrote to Bentley on 17 September 1769[6] saying that painters could complete at most one vase a day 'with a fine subject'. He asked Bentley to collect as many painters as were necessary to decorate a wagon load of vases each week, the quantity that Bentley had said he could sell in London. Josiah thought it might be possible to recruit painters amongst the fan painters or even amongst the coach and house painters, who painted frescoes in the interiors of houses. These people, he felt, would prove better hands than former porcelain painters. He even entertained the idea of founding a painting school, as is evident in a letter to Bentley of 23 May 1770 (E.25-18302):

> I have a *waking notion* haunts me very much of late which is the begining a regular drawing & modeling school to train up artists for ourselves. I wo[d]. pick up some likely Boys of about 12 years old & take them apprentice 'till they are twenty or twenty one & set them to drawing & when they had made some tolerable proficiency they sho[d]. practice with outlines of figures upon Vases which I wo[d]. send you to be fill'd up. We could make out lines which wo[d]. bear carriage & these might tend to facilitate your doing a quantity of the Patent Vases, & when you wanted any hands we could draft them out of this school. 'The Paintings upon these Vases from W & B school' – so it may be s[d]. 1000 years hence. Adieu.

The site of the painting workshop, which from about April 1768 had occupied premises at the Queen's Arms, 1 Great Newport Street, Soho, moved during the next year to a location in Chelsea which can no longer be exactly pin-pointed. According to one writer,[7] it is likely to have been at the east end of the present Upper Cheyne Row and north of a row of houses, numbers 18 to 28. Bentley's house was apparently situated south of King's Road between Glebe Place and Bramerton Street. David Rhodes, the head enameller, moved from St Martin's Lane to a house at 2 Little Cheyne Row (now 26 Upper Cheyne Row) rented for him by Wedgwood and Bentley. The premises in Chelsea were taken before the end of September 1769 and were ready by December when workmen from Etruria came down to London. Some painters from the neighbouring Chelsea China Factory may also have been employed. In May 1774 new showrooms were opened at Portland House, Greek Street, and all the business in London was brought under one roof. Bentley left Chelsea in July 1774 to take up residence at 11 Greek Street, Soho, so that he could supervise the adjoining showroom and enamelling shop. The showrooms were not moved again until 1796, although Bentley went to live at Turnham Green, at least six miles from Soho, in July 1777.

During the hectic period 1769–70 it is clear that a fairly large number of encaustic vases must have been produced and sold by Wedgwood and Bentley. Even after competitors such as Humphrey Palmer of Hanley began making them too, they were still made at Etruria and continued to be a speciality of the firm. The examples in the British Museum collection are not easily datable. The author has taken the quality of the basalt, its silkiness and smoothness, as a guide to the period when the vases in the Museum were made, since it is known that Josiah was always seeking to improve his ceramic bodies. The sharpness of any lathe-turned, or fluted decoration and the clarity of the painting have also been considered, but it should be remembered that not every kiln in Josiah's time would be successfully fired, and that high-quality pieces were made after his death.

One piece, a ewer (Fig. 71), can be dated to about 1775 on the grounds of the similarity of the painting technique employed to that found on a dated basalt vase in the Wedgwood Museum.[8] In addition, the British Museum ewer has a wonderfully smooth body and is crisply finished around the neck. The commemorative vase at Barlaston is inscribed 31 January 1774, the date of the death of Henry Earle, and it was presumably made at about that time. On it and the British Museum ewer a considerable amount of white has been used, and it is slightly shiny in

Figure 71 Black basalt ewer, decorated in encaustic colours with a scene shown in Caylus's *Recueil d'Antiquités*, and engine-turned on neck and foot, unmarked, *c.* 1774. H. 9⅜ in (23.8 cm). Presented by Mr and Mrs Isaac Falcke, 1909.

appearance. The scene on the British Museum ewer, however, is based on a classical source, unlike the decoration on the Henry Earle vase which is typical of memorial pieces made in the eighteenth century in various materials. The charioteer on the Museum vase, shown with his whip raised in his right hand whilst his left holds the neck of one of his two serpent steeds as he drives over an old man holding a club on the ground, is copied exactly from an illustration of a gem in the second volume of Count Caylus's *Receuil d'Antiquités* (see also p. 79).[9] A copy of this work belonged to the Wedgwood and Bentley partnership[10] in 1770. Caylus reports that this subject, which occurs on a finely engraved agate, was a rare one and to his knowledge had never before been published in any book illustrating engraved gems.[11] It was perhaps for this reason that it was chosen by Wedgwood and Bentley who probably admired the vigorous and unusual scene.

More typical of encaustic-painted basalt production are pieces decorated in matt red on black. These imitated the Greek red-figure vases, a number of which were in the British Museum by 1772 and were acknowledged by cultivated minds as national treasures. A ewer (Pl. 6b) of the same form as the preceding piece but slightly larger is also unmarked and therefore is only provisionally datable. The flattened part of the vase between body and neck is less finely formed than that of the previous piece, where it has been carefully fluted, and in addition its surface does not have a polished appearance. The scene of a bull with two women is taken from an illustration depicting a marriage ceremony in the second volume of Hamilton's *Antiquities* (pl. 45),[12] and has been cleverly adapted to the shape of the basalt piece. It is likely that it dates from between 1769, when Wedgwood first mentions using d'Hancarville's book on Hamilton's collection as a source for painting on basalt pieces[13] and about 1780 when Bentley died.

From the same period are two small vases with twisted rope handles (Pl. 6b), their shape based on the Greek neck amphora. Prior to the Falcke Gift these vases were the only examples of encaustic painting on Wedgwood's basalt in the British Museum collection, with the exception of the unusual plaque discussed on p. 94. Given the great tradition of collecting classical antiquities in the Museum which dates back to the earliest years of the institution, this failure to assemble a representative group of Wedgwood's 'interpretations' of Greek red-figure vases is altogether remarkable. The subjects on the small vases, Psyche binding Cupid and Cupid Bound, depicted in sepia tones, are copied from illustrations in a work by Antonio Francesco Gori published in 1731 illustrating engraved gems in Florentine gem cabinets.[14] An illustration of a dancing cupid in the same work[15] is similar to but not identical with the subject shown on a two-handled vase (Pl. 6b). Its shape, unlike that of the preceding pair of vases, is based on a classical prototype which is shown in the first volume of Hamilton's *Antiquities*,[16] but in this instance, as in many others, adaptations have been made. Wedgwood's vase shows a disregard for accurate use of his classical sources which typified the neoclassical movement. Vases like these could cost from a guinea to ten or twelve guineas each on the evidence of catalogues issued by the firm.

Basalt was normally used for ornamental pieces, and it is reasonable to suppose that the small cup and saucer with encaustic painting of trophies of love and music (Pl. 6b) were intended as 'cabinet pieces' for display rather than use. They have different impressed marks but must belong together because their motifs, such as the horn and the torch, and the bow and quiver tied with a ribbon, match so closely, and their border decoration of stylised leaf and berry trails is identical. They were probably made at the end of the eighteenth or possibly at the beginning of the nineteenth century. The appearance of the basalt is noticeably less fine than the body of the ewers mentioned earlier.

A pair of basalt flower vases of *kantharos* shape, each with the addition of a detachable pierced flower holder and a lid designed to rest on a ledge inside (Pl.

6b), date from after Josiah's death. Their stylised classical ornament is painted in rather flat-looking encaustic colours, and the basalt is very different from the silky polished material of the 1770s. The shape of the vases reveals that enthusiasm for European interpretations or copies of classical antiquities endured over several decades.

Vases were, of course, the most commonly produced items decorated in the encaustic technique. Flat pieces, however, were also manufactured, although they do appear to be quite rare. A small oval basalt plaque enclosed in a finely worked metal frame which is likely to be contemporary (Pl. 6b) is painted with a subject which can probably be identified as either a 'Quadriga' or a 'Charioteer' in the section entitled 'Encaustic Painting' in the catalogue of the sale held in December 1781 in order to dispose of the goods belonging to the partnership. No. 845 in the catalogue is listed as 'A Suité [sic] of three ditto [i.e. 'Tablets for Pictures'] Victory, Quadriga, Charioteer'. A note in ink in the copy of the catalogue held in the Library of the Department of Medieval and Later Antiquities in the British Museum records that the lot fetched 9 guineas. There are no details given in the 1773 catalogue of the subjects painted on tablets 'of the artificial Basaltes', so the plaque may perhaps be dated between around 1773 and 1781. Probably intended to be hung on the wall in exactly the same way as a picture, its subject was copied from an illustration of an engraved carnelian entitled 'Quadriga' which appears as an unnumbered plate in Pietro Santi Bartoli's *Raccolta di Camei e Gemmi Antiche* published in Rome in 1727.[17] The gem was then in the renowned Odescalchi collection. The same subject, slightly differently interpreted, appears on an engraved sard from the cabinet of Baron Morpeth engraved by Picart in 1722.[18]

The most unusual piece of painted basalt in the British Museum is without doubt the plaque with a sacrifice scene within an oval reserve (Pl. 6a). The precise meaning of this highly symbolic scene has not yet been discovered, but one suggestion is that the male term being garlanded by a nymph at the left stands for the creative arts, also symbolised by the three putti at the foot of the term. One of these shown seated and in the act of painting is an allegory of the arts; another with a torch may stand for love; whilst the third with its cornucopia bestows fertility on love. The mysterious seated female to the right of the scene with her staff and book symbolises reflection, and possibly learning.[19] The decorative scene is based on an engraving by Bartolozzi after a painting by Cipriani (1727–85) which is thought to date from around 1775.[20] The neoclassical border decoration of anthemions enclosed within the 'frame' surrounding the scene is almost certainly adapted from illustrations in Hamilton's *Antiquities* where it is found in many variations in red and black. The source of the rosettes in each corner of the plaque, which is one of the few places where the basalt can be seen, is not known. The same palette of matt pale grey-blue, white and sepia was used on other comparable pieces, which are few in number.[21] All are decorated with classically inspired scenes or with motifs based on classical engraved gems. The painting of the whole group may have been carried out by the same artist, but so far he or she has not been identified.

Before discussing an example of encaustic-painted caneware in the neoclassical style, another unusual flat painted piece must be mentioned. This circular plaque has on the reverse an unglazed band which was perhaps a foot rim, or even a stem (Figs 72, 73), and there are two holes in the rim which show that it was intended for suspension. There is some argument as to whether these holes were drilled before or after firing, but the probability is that they were made after the plaque had been glazed since the glaze would not otherwise be chipped away round the holes but would come right up to their edges. The painting, which is not particularly skilful, is generally dated to the late eighteenth century. Executed in enamels over the glaze, it is rendered in an almost monochrome palette in a technique

Figure 72 Creamware plaque
painted in sepia with Cleopatra
before Augustus after a painting by Angelica Kauffmann
(1741–1807), engraved by
Thomas Burke, impressed
WEDGWOOD and incised marks,
c. 1786. Diam. 12⅛ in (30.7 cm).
Presented by Mr and Mrs
Isaac Falcke, 1909.

Figure 73 Reverse of creamware plaque (Fig. 72) showing
impressed and incised marks
and remains of a possible foot
rim.

95

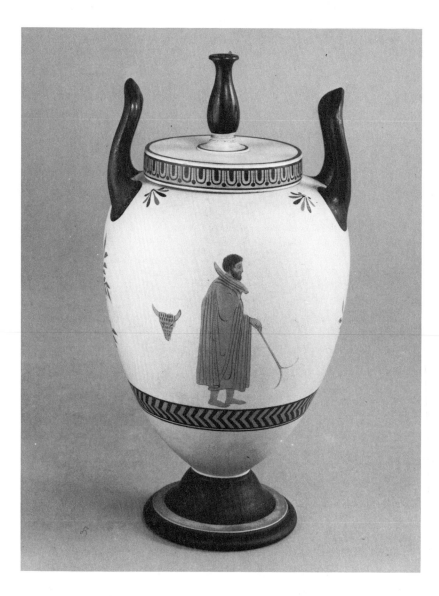

Figure 74 Caneware two-handled vase and cover decorated in black and red-brown encaustic colours with an athletic trainer and a bull's head copied from illustrations in Hamilton's *Antiquities*, impressed WEDGWOOD, A, c. 1785–95. H. 7⅝ in (19.5 cm). Presented by Mr and Mrs Isaac Falcke, 1909.

which is sometimes described as *grisaille*. Only brown and white pigments have been used to reproduce a scene of Cleopatra before Augustus, probably based on an engraving published by Thomas Burke (1749–1815) in 1786 after a painting by Angelica Kauffmann (1741–1807).[22] This Swiss artist came to England in the mid-1760s and in 1768 was one of the founder members, with Sir Joshua Reynolds, of the Royal Academy. Her paintings in the neoclassical style attained considerable popularity and hold a special fascination for the potters who had them copied on to their ornamental pieces, sometimes even including Kauffmann's signature and thus giving rise to misapprehensions in the minds of later collectors.

The figure of Cleopatra on this plaque is reasonably well executed, although slightly out of proportion, but the two standing figures are stiff and even the furnishings which provide the 'classical' setting are poorly painted. No alternative attribution has yet been made to take the place of the suggestion[23] that the plaque may have been painted by William Hopkins Craft. However, if it were decorated after Burke's engraving, that is around 1786, then it is less likely that Craft painted it since he is referred to in Wedgwood's letters some sixteen years earlier. No evidence has been found to show that he continued to work for Wedgwood over a long period. Yet the style of the figures on the British Museum plaque bears some relationship to those on a signed enamel plaque by Craft dated 1782 depicting 'The Judgement of Paris' after Kauffmann.[24] The creamware plaque is a most exceptional piece. Few examples of eighteenth-century figure-painting from the Wedgwood factory are known and detailed research on them has still to be undertaken.

An ornamental vase and cover of caneware painted in black and red-brown in the encaustic technique is one of the masterpieces of the British Museum collection (Pl. 13, Fig. 74). Its shape is closely based on a fourth-century BC south Italian *lebes gamikos* (marriage bowl),[25] and it corresponds in general outline to the three vases making up a silver condiment set of 1771–2 which was the work of the London silversmiths Louisa Courtauld and George Cowles.[26] The silver vases are more pointed at their lower ends, have additional ornament on the feet, covers and finials and larger handles, but there is an undoubted relationship between them and the Wedgwood vase and cover. The first owner of the silver vases, Lord Curzon of Kedleston Hall, is referred to in Josiah's correspondence, and documents may one day enable scholars to pin down the precise connection between these objects.

The painted decoration of the vase and cover, as so often on the unglazed wares, is once again copied from a piece illustrated in the second volume of Hamilton's *Antiquities*.[27] The man with the forked stick can be seen in his proper role as an athletic trainer on a red-figure south Italian bell *krater* (now in the Department of Greek and Roman Antiquities in the British Museum) dating from the late fifth century BC and painted by the so-called Cyclops Painter.[28] The addition of the isolated bull's head shows that the potter (or the painter) was not afraid to combine motifs taken from different places. The head is shown in another illustration from the same volume.[29] The female figure on the other side also appears in Hamilton's *Antiquities*.[30] Like other vases already mentioned this one may well have been intended to stand on a mantelpiece; no other similar ones are recorded.

The production of useful wares decorated with hand-painted motifs continued side by side with the more showy ornamental pieces. These domestic creamwares, which proved to have a perennial appeal, were made over a long period so dating is open to some debate.

A pair of two-handled custard cups painted with grape and vine leaf decoration (Fig. 75) are of a type that enjoyed long-lasting popularity. They formed part of a dessert service and were made in sets of six with a matching tray. They continued in production up to the beginning of the present century. The moulded shape of these cups owes a debt to the art of the metal worker whilst the overall conception probably derived from a French porcelain prototype. The painting, although it lacks individuality, was nevertheless the work of a skilled artist as it is competently and cleanly executed.

Another category of painting on domestic wares which is of some rarity is the reproduction of motifs taken from Hamilton's *Antiquities* on creamware plates and dishes which may or may not have been intended for use. To the author's knowledge this kind of decoration does not occur on pieces such as tureens or sauceboats, although a shaped dish in the British Museum collection painted in the same manner in orange and black with a classical-style vessel in the centre is of the form illustrated in the firm's pattern books as a stand for a sauceboat.[31] Of the three remaining plates in the collection only one can be included (Fig. 76). It shows the central figure in an illustration in the first volume of Hamilton's

Antiquities[32] which depicts the painted scene on a famous Athenian red-figured vase known as the Meidias *hydria*. This vase has been in the British Museum since 1772. The painting on it shows the rape of the daughters of Leukippos in the sanctuary of Aphrodite, and the figure Josiah Wedgwood chose to depict on the pearlware plate is Aphrodite herself.

In this instance the painter has not provided any support for the lady who, apart from a small pole she may be resting on, is shown suspended in mid-air. On the Pegasus Vase (see Chapter 5), however, a scene on another Greek vase where a seated female is shown has been adapted so that she is provided with a seat. The tomb against which she rests in the Hamilton illustration has been suppressed by the painter of the Wedgwood plate. The anthemion border decoration on the plate was also copied from motifs in d'Hancarville's publication. These plates are usually dated to about 1775–80. Many of the series have letters painted in black on the reverse which may be unidentified painter's marks. The work is certainly of a high order, despite the fact that one palmette has been omitted on the border of the piece illustrated.

One of the greatest achievements of the factory in both its branches was the massive dinner and dessert service of cream-coloured earthenware ordered in 1773 by the Russian Empress Catherine II through Alexander Baxter, the Russian Consul in London. Wedgwood and Bentley were themselves extremely proud of this service and made a catalogue of it when it was completed. Each piece was to be painted with the device of the green frog standing for the palace built on the Frog Marsh (near Petrodvorets, about five miles from Leningrad) in honour of the Empress's lover, Grigori Orlov. The service was intended for fifty persons and consisted originally of 952 pieces. It was hand painted with topographical views of Great Britain, some of picturesque scenes of ruins or castles often after prints collected and issued in the various editions published over several decades from 1726 to 1752 of Nathaniel Buck's *Antiquities* or Francis Grose's *Antiquities of England and Wales*.[33] These two volumes of prints had been particularly appreciated by connoisseurs of the preceding generation.

A rare dessert plate from this service, most of which survives in the State

Hermitage Museum, Leningrad,[34] where a portion of it is exhibited, is numbered 190 on the reverse in brownish-black enamel (Pl. 4). This plate is one of the treasures of the British Museum and was reidentified by Hugh Tait in 1969, as depicting a view of Mr Hopkins's Gardens at Painshill, Surrey.[35] The gardens, devised by Mr Charles Hamilton, and referred to by Horace Walpole in his *Observations on Modern Gardening*,[36] were in existence until World War II. The view shown on the dessert plate has been copied from a print, first published in 1760,[37] entitled 'A View from the West Side of the Island in the Garden of the Honble. Charles Hamilton Esqr., at Painshill, near Cobham in Surry' by W. Wollett. The view is repeated on an oval dish from the dinner service numbered 304, still in the Hermitage Museum, and it seems likely that the plate now in the British Museum, being a duplicate, never left England. Another view of Painshill appears on a plate from the dinner service numbered 143 and on part of the cover of a dish numbered 599. Yet another plate from the dinner service has a view of 'a ruin on Mr Hopkins' property at Painshill, Surrey'.[38] The history of the Museum plate is unknown; it was presented in 1898 by F. B. Goldney without any note of its provenance.

About thirty-three enamellers in all were employed on the decoration of this service, and work commenced at Chelsea on 3 April 1773. Some details of the painters who worked on the service and the wages they were paid can be found in archival sources; this and other information has been published in Dr G. C. Williamson's account[39] which appeared in 1909 to coincide with the showing in London of forty-nine pieces lent from St Petersburg by Tsar Nicholas II. The

Painting on 18th-century Wedgwood

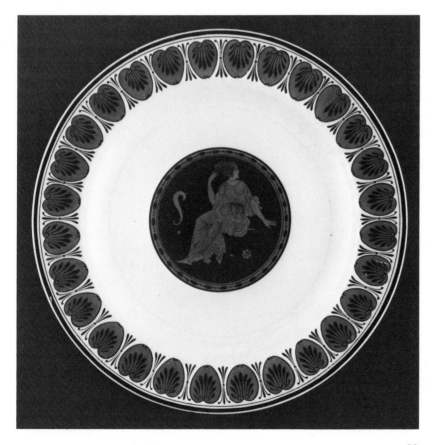

Figure 76 Creamware plate painted in red and orange with Aphrodite taken from a representation of the Meidias *hydria* in Hamilton's *Antiquities*, impressed WEDGWOOD, R, *c.* 1775–80. Note the unfinished anthemion motif in the border. Diam. 8⅛ in (20.7 cm). Presented by Mr and Mrs Isaac Falcke, 1909.

frogs are recorded as being painted by Nathaniel Cooper, who also decorated the borders, at $2\frac{1}{2}d$ to $3d$ each, presumably according to size. The edges also had to be painted, a task carried out by Samuel Armstrong. Amongst the landscape painters were Miss Glisson, who was paid 12s a week, and Miss Pars, who was paid 10s 6d per week and may have specialised in painting ruins. She lived with her brother, William Pars, who was also a painter and Associate of the Royal Academy, in Cheyne Row, Chelsea. Mr and Mrs Wilcox, whose names are frequently mentioned in Wedgwood's letters to Bentley, tackled borders and landscapes respectively. Mrs Wilcox was paid 18s per week. The total cost of the decorative work amounted to the considerable sum of £2,300, which was broken down in Wedgwood's accounting to £1,306 for the views of which there were 1,244, and £933 for the borders and frogs. The cost of the undecorated pieces was insignificant and the profit on the service negligible.

However, the service created a sensation in London where Wedgwood decided as early as November 1773 to exhibit it. By 31 May 1774 the showrooms in Greek Street, Soho, had been prepared and advertisements placed in the *Public Advertiser*.[40] From the first week of June the service was on display for about two months and was seen by Queen Charlotte and her brother Ernest of Mecklenburgh in mid-July.[41] On 8 July Wedgwood asked Bentley to make arrangements for the transport of the service to Russia. By October it had arrived and been paid for, despite Wedgwood's fears at the outset that he might never receive payment. It was shown to the Ambassador to the Court of St Petersburg, Sir James Harris, and he wrote to his father on 3 June 1779[42] in terms that lead us to believe that Catherine was proud of the service.

> I have the good fortune to have made myself not disagreeable to the Empress. She notices me much more than any of my colleagues, more, I believe, than any stranger is used to. She admits me to all her parties of cards, and a few days ago carried me with only two of her courtiers to a country palace, where she has placed portraits of all the crowned heads of Europe. We discussed much on their several merits, and still more on the great demerits of the modern portrait-painters, since in the whole collection, except one of our two eldest princes, done by West, there is not a single picture that has either design, colour, or composition. She calls this place *la Grenouilliere*; and it was for it that Wedgewood [sic] made, some years ago, a very remarkable service of his ware, on which a green frog was painted. It represented the different country houses and gardens in England. This, also, we were shown, and this led us to a conversation on English gardening in which the Empress is a great adept.

There has always been an element of mystery surrounding the presence in the West of pieces from the 'Frog Service'. From Williamson's account it is fairly clear that the service was considered of no importance as a work of art towards the end of the Tsarist era. Its exact location was probably known only to a few members of the Imperial staff, since it took Dr Williamson some time to obtain information about it. However, British interest soon aroused its counterpart in St Petersburg, where an article on the service appeared in the progressive art magazine *Stariye Gody* in February 1910. There is always the possibility that a few pieces left Russia at some time after the death of the Empress and the reawakening of interest in the service in the early twentieth century. The other explanation of the presence of examples in the West is that they were never sent abroad. A letter of 20 and 21 June 1774 from Wedgwood to Bentley (E.25-18540) is evidence that some pieces at least never left this country:

> I should be glad to have a few duplicates of the Russian service sent to Etruria next Monday. The Soup Plate of Ld Gowers, & a few other *good ones*, Dishes &c., none of the slight ordinary things, they will not be worth shewing. I think the *fine painted* pieces condemn'd to be set aside whether it be on account of their being blister'd, duplicates, or any other fault, *except poor & bad painting*, should be divided between Mr Baxter & Etruria, & we may paint more *without the Frog*, to be shewn in Greek Street.

A recent acquisition can perhaps be connected with the group of pieces without the frog ordered by Wedgwood. It is a creamware plate with the border decoration as found on the dessert service supplied to the Empress Catherine, and decorated in colours with a view of 'Westcowes Castle, in the Isle of Wight' (Pl. 5). This charming and tranquil scene is based on a print engraved by Ellis from a drawing by Francis Grose made in 1761 which appeared as an unnumbered plate (it is in fact pl. 4) published on 1 October 1772 in the second volume of Grose's *The Antiquities of England and Wales* (1774). The rowing boat in the water and the broken-up pieces of timber have been added and something which may be a haystack near the cannon has been omitted by the painter. The castle is described by Grose as having been built by Henry VIII in about 1539 slightly to the west of the town, that is, West Cowes, guarding the entrance to Newport River. This castle, and the one on the opposite shore at East Cowes, were in ruins at the time of the fourth edition of Camden's *Britannia* in 1722, almost forty years before Grose drew the site. Little remains now of Henry VIII's castle, as it is called by Nikolaus Pevsner and David Lloyd in their 1967 edition of *Hampshire and the Isle of Wight*, and nothing at all of East Cowes Castle. A similar scene is painted in monochrome on a soup plate numbered 455 in the dinner service at the Hermitage Museum, differing only in the details of the shore and the trees in front of the castle. The polychrome plate in the British Museum is slightly smaller than the 'Frog' plate, measuring $8\frac{7}{8}$ in (22.3 cm) instead of $9\frac{3}{4}$ in (24.8 cm) in diameter. Found by chance in the Isle of Wight, its previous history is at present unknown. Other polychrome pieces belong to the Wedgwood family, and five of these are displayed at the Wedgwood Museum, Barlaston,[43] whilst a handful of examples can be found in public and private collections in the USA and Canada. It is unlikely that their exact purpose will ever be known unless as yet undiscovered documentary evidence comes to light.

The British Museum is the only public collection in Britain with examples of both the monochrome and the polychrome painting associated with the creamware service ordered by Catherine the Great.

5 The Pegasus Vase

Not long before Wedgwood embarked on copying the Roman glass Portland Vase in jasper ware (see Chapter 6), he completed a rather less famous vase, presenting an example of it to the British Museum. It is now known as the Pegasus Vase (Pl. 10) from the moulded figure of the flying horse surmounting the cover, although in the nineteenth century it was commonly referred to as the 'Homeric Vase' on account of the scene on one side of the vase which shows the so-called 'Apotheosis of Homer'. The scene is occasionally dubbed the 'Crowning of a Kitharist' since the central figure, a bearded man (previously thought to represent the famous Greek poet), resting his left foot on the lower step of a two-tiered structure, supports on his left hip an instrument with eight strings known in Greek as a *kithara*.[1] He holds a plectrum in his left hand and is clothed in a long flowing garment (*chiton*) over which is a shorter one (*chiton schistos*). Facing him is a victory (or *nike*) with outstretched wings holding out both hands to him as if offering him something. She seems to have just alighted on the lower step of the podium, but only one foot is shown and her attitude is hard to interpret. Just behind her is a seated bearded man (in Greek *agonothetes*) wearing a long mantle, with a wreath around his forehead, presiding over the festivities from his chair. On the left is a seated female figure balancing a long spear against her left shoulder, and above her is a *nike* in flight descending towards the kitharist with a bowl-like object in her left hand (a fluted *phiale* placed in another *phiale* decorated with circles). Her right hand is outstretched, and the many folds of her Doric *chiton* and *shendone* are carefully shown, copied faithfully from the Greek original.

On the other side of the vase is a much less unified design showing, almost beneath the mask of Medusa at the base of one of the handles, a basin (similar to the Greek *loutron*) on a fluted foot (corresponding to the Greek *hyper-staton*) beside which are flower garlands (Fig. 77). On the left is a figure of Minerva standing inside a temple-like building with her right hand raised. Next is a large palm-tree with a ridged trunk and feathery leaves which reach almost as high as the top of the body of the vase (Fig. 78). On the left almost beneath the mask at the base of the other handle is a small altar with a laurel branch at either side (Fig. 79). The handles themselves are formed of the heads and necks of two serpents of white jasper ware whose mouths close over a pale blue jasper ware egg. A Medusa mask on a ground composed of scales has writhing snakes for hair and conceals the attachments of the handles to the vase. Each mask is of white jasper ware.

The dome-shaped lid is ornamented in white jasper near the rim with a pattern loosely based on a classical motif. The edge of the upper part of the lid has been lathe-turned (Fig. 80). The pale blue cloud on which the white jasper figure of the horse rests appears to have been hand-modelled. Examination of the interior of the lid suggests that a hole was cut in the peak of the dome and a lump of pale blue

Figure 77 View of the blue jasper vase and cover known as the Pegasus Vase showing handle formed of two snakes biting an egg, with Medusa mask terminal; below a basin or *loutron*, to the left the figure of Minerva standing in a niche. Reliefs and handles in white jasper, egg in serpents' mouths pale blue jasper. Presented by Josiah Wedgwood, 1786. Total H. 18¼ in (46.4 cm). Total L. of base 6¼ in (15.9 cm).

Figure 78 (*overleaf*) Reverse of the Pegasus Vase. The design is far less unified than the scene on the other side (see Pl. 10) copied directly from Hamilton's *Antiquities*.

Figure 79 (*page 105*) Side of the Pegasus Vase showing the rather isolated altar framed by laurel bushes.

103

clay put over the top and then carefully modelled by the craftsman. The figure
of the horse was probably made in a two-part mould, but the seamline is almost
invisible. The wings, mane and other details have been tooled. The base is
impressed with the potter's name and with two leaf-like marks (Fig. 81), perhaps
those of the craftsman responsible for forming the vase, its lid, foot and base.
All except the last were thrown on the wheel. The base is made of five flat rectangular pieces of clay joined together when in the leather-hard state with water.

All the reliefs on the body of the vase are white, whilst the body itself is a pale,
almost greyish, blue. This vase, including its base and cover, stands $18\frac{1}{4}$ in
(46.4 cm) in height and is a triumph of the potter's art. Here and there the reliefs
have buckled slightly in the firing and become detached from the body, to which
they were fixed with water after being removed from the mould in which they
were made. The body itself is ovoid in shape but flattened at the top, and con-
forms in general outline to the Greek *stamnos*. It is almost imperceptibly warped;
however, the general impression is of a crisply executed vase of impressive
proportions.

Josiah's own enthusiasm for the vase seems genuine. He referred to it in a
(draft) letter to Sir William Hamilton written on 24 June 1786 (E.26-18976)
when concluding a request for advice about the Portland Vase. Having mentioned
an order for jasper wares received from the King of Naples which is to be shipped
by a Manchester merchant, he ends his letter by saying: 'I lamented much that I
could not obtain liberty of the mercht. to send a vase, the finest & most perfect
I have ever made, & which I have since presented to the British Museum. I
inclose a rough sketch of it: it is 18 inches high & the price 20 guineas.' At the
foot of the page is a note: 'The sketch of the vase could not be got ready for this

post but shall be sent soon: Subject, the apotheosis of Homer.' The British
Museum records show that, according to the Minutes of the General Meeting
held on 27 May 1786, Wedgwood had recently presented 'a Vase of his own
manufacture' and was to be thanked by the Trustees who accepted it. As items of
contemporary manufacture were not generally taken into the collections, it must
indeed have been much admired.

As he was soon to do with the Portland Vase, Josiah relied heavily on inspiration from the ancient world when he created the Pegasus Vase, but it is an
adaptation from various sources rather than a direct copy. The main scene on the
vase was originally adapted by the young John Flaxman (who was aged twenty-
three at the time) for a jasper ware plaque intended for incorporation into mantelpieces. An extract from a letter dated 26 February 1779 to Sir William Hamilton
in Thomas Bentley's hand shows how Flaxman worked:[2]

His Excellency Sir Wm Hamilton at Naples
Sir
Having modelled a large Tablet from one of the unpublished Designs in your Excellency's Collection at the British Museum which we copied from a drawing lent us by M^r
D'Hancarville, and which we consider as one of the most perfect Specimens of the
present State of our Ornamental Manufactory, we could not resist the desire of presenting
you with a Coppy [sic] of this Work, which has come very happily thro' the fiery Trial,
and which we hope you will do us the Honour to place in your Cabinet, or in some of
your Apartments.

We understand the Subject to be some Honour paid to the Genius of Homer: but perhaps
your Excellency will have the Goodness to inform us more exactly what this fine Composition represents, and who the venerable Person is that sits listening with so much
Pleasure to the Music of the Bard?

Hamilton did not write to thank the potter and his partner until 22 June (E.32-
5365) when he acknowledged the receipt of 'your Delightfull Basrelief of the
Apotheose of Homer, or some celebrated Poet indeed it is far superior to my
most sanguine expectation . . .'. He concludes his letter: 'Your Basrelief
astonishes all the artists here, it is more pure & in a truer antique Taste than any
of their performances tho' they have so many fine models before them.'

Although the name of John Flaxman jun. is not mentioned by Bentley in the
letter quoted above, a letter written by Sir William Hamilton to Josiah Wedgwood from Naples on 24 July 1786[3] in reply to the potter's request for advice on
how to copy the Portland Vase provides proof that the young sculptor was in fact
responsible for the adaptation of the classical scene for Wedgwood's purposes, as
the connoisseur writes: 'I should have thought my friend Flaxman would
have been of use to you in your present undertaking, for I must do him the
justice to say, I never saw a bas-relief executed in the true simple antique style
half so well as that he did of the Apotheosis of Homer from one of my vases . . .'

The vase in question, which had been acquired by Hamilton in Italy, then sold
by him to the British Museum in 1763, is a painted earthenware Greek *kalyx
krater* of the finest style now thought to date from the fourth century BC.[4] Subtle
alterations to the scene as shown in d'Hancarville's publication (Fig. 82) had to
be made by Flaxman as the jasper ware medium could not accurately reproduce
some details found on the painted vase. For instance, the musical instrument is
differently interpreted because of the nature of the ceramic medium, and the
strings are shown attached at the top in a way that would render them unplayable.
The seated female holds her spear on her right side on the painted vase and on
careful examination is shown to be suspended in mid-air in a sitting position.
Since the eighteenth-century mind was much more literal Flaxman had to supply
a stool for her. As to the figure in the temple, representations of Minerva appear
in many of the works on classical art which the potter is known to have owned.

The figure is based on the Minerva Giustiniani, now in the Vatican Museum.[5] Representations of palm trees are not especially rare in classical art, but none has yet been discovered in the eighteenth-century collections of engravings such as de Montfaucon's work[6] which parallels the ridged trunk and feathery leaves shown on the reverse of the vase. The small altar is reminiscent of altars painted on fourth-century BC classical vases from Greece and south Italy, but no eighteenth-century printed source has been traced. The handle terminals were copied from an illustration of a sandal shown in de Montfaucon where the Medusa head appears as an ornament (Fig. 83). The rather unhappy combination of such ill-assorted decorative elements suggests that the design was the work of one of the factory's modellers, rather than one of the artists employed by Wedgwood.

The history of the making of the Pegasus Vase was until quite recently a complete mystery: it appeared that no records had survived of the manufacture of this model, a strange omission in view of Wedgwood's delight in it. However, recent work on the 'Oven Books', or records of firings kept at the factory,[7] has brought to light the following information. Under the date '18 and 25 February' 1786 is the curious entry 'two blue & white vases 23 Ins with palm tree angel temple &c'. This unlikely description of the Pegasus Vase, lacking any illustration in the left-hand margin (which has been torn), is the first-known mention of the production of the vase. There is another entry in the book for '4 and 11 March': '2 fine white jasper vases 23Ins diped. Made thrown, turned & finished & broke/? . . . angels &c on'. The shape number is given as '298'. Although an entry dated '1 and 8 September' records the firing of '1 white odd cover to an Apotheosis' and '6 blue & white vases 20Ins high' with the shape number 298 appear on '15 & 22 September', there is no other blue example resembling the vase in the British

Figure 82 Pl. 31, from vol. 3 of Hamilton's *Antiquities*. The coloured engraving representing figures on a Greek red-figure vase of the finest period was adapted by John Flaxman jun., first for a plaque and later for one side of the Pegasus Vase. Note that the figure at the left is sitting suspended in mid-air. The design around the edge has been adapted for use as relief ornament on the lid of the vase. Copyright British Library.

Museum known to the author. Still others may have been produced, but the factory records do not survive for the period shortly after 1786.

There are, however, other eighteenth-century examples of the vase in existence. Perhaps the most well-known is a green jasper dip one in the Felix Joseph Collection at the Nottingham Castle Museum.[8] The concealment of the fixture of the vase to its base differs from that of the British Museum vase, although the actual method of fixing may well be the same. Inside the Nottingham vase is a white jasper ware dome, about 2 in (5 cm) in height, covering the fitment. On the British Museum vase the fitment has been left exposed inside a $1\frac{1}{2}$-in (3.8-cm)-deep well formed of blue jasper ware. It seems to be made of some kind of glue or mastic, and is dark brown in colour.[9] A blue jasper dip Pegasus Vase, $17\frac{5}{8}$ in (44.5 cm) high and lacking the square base usually associated with the piece, is in the Wedgwood Museum at Barlaston.[10] There are some minor differences between it and the British Museum vase, including the arrangement of the ornamental reliefs around the foot. The figure of Minerva in the temple is missing, possibly indicating a date of manufacture after Josiah I's death, as this feature is noticeable on many examples which were clearly made in the nineteenth century, and the author conjectures that the mould for this figure could have been lost at some time.

Besides other jasper ware versions of the vase, some of them of undoubted nineteenth-century manufacture, there are also a small number of black basalt examples of differing dimensions. One of these is a monumental vase, cover and pedestal in the British Museum collection (Fig. 84).[11] It bears the impressed mark WEDGWOOD and two workman's marks, one of which is T, probably for the workman responsible for the piece. The pedestal is ornamented with vine swags and ribbons in relief. There is no figure of Minerva in the temple on the 'reverse' of the vase. Written in pencil inside the lid is 'Exhibited/South Kensington Museum/February 20/76'. At this time (1876) the vase belonged to Mr and Mrs Isaac Falcke.

The blue jasper ware Pegasus Vase in the British Museum has unique historical associations (as already mentioned, it was one of the earliest pieces of 'modern' ceramics to enter the collection) and seems to be the only example of the famous vase which can be securely dated to the late eighteenth century. Today few examples ever appear in the salerooms and unlike the Portland Vase, which was produced in considerable quantities in the nineteenth century and later, it has never been manufactured in large numbers, although copies could be ordered

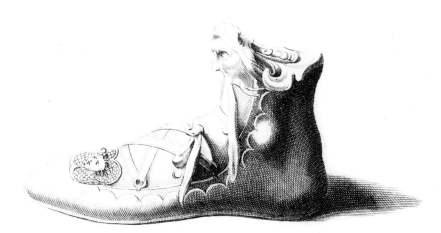

Figure 83 Pl. 34, from vol. 3, part 1 of Montfaucon's *L' Antiquité Expliquée et Représentée en Figures*, showing a sandal with an ornament near the toe copied by Josiah Wedgwood and used as a handle terminal for the Pegasus Vase. Copyright British Library.

Figure 84 Black basalt
Pegasus Vase and stand,
impressed WEDGWOOD and
with impressed workman's
marks, mid-19th century.
Total H. 27¼ in (69 cm). H. of
vase and cover 14¾ in (37.5 cm).
Presented by Mr and Mrs
Isaac Falcke, 1909.

early this century.[12] The Museum vase, which is notable for its silky surface, crisp reliefs and distinctive outline, is a reminder of the excellence achieved by the potter. Characteristically Josiah Wedgwood wished his achievement to be demonstrated to the world at large. This generous gift to the Museum, accepted by the Archbishop of Canterbury and his fellow Trustees and recorded in the Minutes of the General Meeting of 27 May 1786, received only the tersest of acknowledgements: 'Mr Wedgewood [*sic*] having presented a Vase of his own manufacture, thanks were ordered to be returned for the same.'

The Pegasus Vase marked the corner-stone of what was to become one of the finest collections of eighteenth-century Wedgwood. At the beginning of the nineteenth century it was probably displayed next to the blue jasper copy of the Portland Vase presented by John Wedgwood in the Saloon, or Second Antiquity Room, 'on the Top of the Case near the Windows'. 'Two Vases made by Wedgwood; one of them being a Copy of the Barberini or Portland Vase' are recorded in this place in a manuscript list of locations of objects[13] which is undated but is written on paper bearing a watermark for the year 1805. The same vases were on show together 100 years later, as we know from a Museum publication issued in 1904.[14] Wedgwood's Portland and Pegasus Vases are still regularly exhibited side by side.

During all this time the Pegasus Vase has left the British Museum only twice to be shown elsewhere – in 1978 it was displayed at the Science Museum, South Kensington, for an exhibition entitled 'Josiah Wedgwood: The Arts and Sciences United'; and in 1979 it was included in the exhibition organised by the British Council, 'John Flaxman R.A.' which was sent to Hamburg and Copenhagen before arriving at the Royal Academy, London. The vase must certainly be counted amongst the masterpieces of Wedgwood's art.

6 The Portland Vase

Wedgwood's success in copying in his black jasper ware the classical cameo-glass vase commonly known as the Portland Vase (Pl. 9) is frequently regarded as his crowning achievement. Indeed, a representation of the vase has been used as a printed back stamp for bone china by the firm of Josiah Wedgwood and Sons Ltd ever since 1878. Classical vases, especially those acquired by Sir William Hamilton and purchased from him by the British Museum in 1772, were a rich source of inspiration to Josiah Wedgwood, but it is doubtful whether he ever had occasion to study any of them at such close range as he examined the Portland Vase.

The vase, formed of cobalt-blue glass (which looks black unless seen by transmitted light) with reliefs in miky-white glass, has always attracted public attention. It must be one of the most famous and yet most mysterious pieces of classical art, and its history and iconography have been the subject of endless studies. Housed in the British Museum since 1810 when it was deposited on loan by the Fourth Duke of Portland, it was not actually purchased from the Portland family until 1945. It has been on permanent exhibition during all those years except for three from 1929 to 1932, when it was put up for sale at Christie's but failed to reach its reserve, and for shorter periods when it was undergoing restoration.

Restoration of the vase was first necessary in 1845 after it had been smashed into many fragments by an inebriated Irishman, William Lloyd. In 1948, three years after its purchase, it was taken to pieces and restored again using new methods and materials. The vase was published on behalf of the British Museum in 1964 by D. E. L. Haynes,[1] then Keeper of Greek and Roman Antiquities, and a revised edition appeared in 1975. This excellent monograph remains the most comprehensive recent publication, although scholars have since challenged Haynes's interpretation of the scenes, and the vase itself has been closely examined again to discover more about its technique of manufacture.[2]

Briefly, the vase is now thought to have been made early in the reign of Augustus, in the decade around 25 BC,[3] probably in Rome by craftsmen who may have been trained in Alexandria, Egypt, where the cameo-glass technique is likely to have originated. The foot of the vase is broken off and the cameo disc, now displayed separately, certainly does not belong, although it was attached to the vessel at least from the early seventeenth century and perhaps even in antiquity. The disc (Fig. 85) itself is cut down from a larger composition, probably a plaque. The colour does not match that of the vase, and the style of the carving suggests that it is slightly later, probably dating from the first quarter of the first century AD.

The disc shows the upper part of a figure of a young man in profile to the right, with his fingers to his lips, wearing a Phrygian cap. He has been identified as Paris, son of King Priam of Troy. After awarding the golden apple to Aphrodite as the fairest of the three goddesses at the wedding feast of Peleus and Thetis,

Figure 85 Base of black jasper ware copy of the Portland Vase. The relief is generally identified as Paris. Near the remains of the old exhibition label the pocking of the surface is especially noticeable. Diam. 5 in (12.8 cm). Presented by Mr and Mrs Isaac Falke, 1909.

Paris seduced Helen with Aphrodite's help, thus setting off the train of events which led to the Trojan War. The fact that this theme is related to that of the vase must be a coincidence.

Most interpretations now identify the myth of Peleus and Thetis on the vase; yet while Haynes reads the two sides together, others see them as illustrating individual but complementary episodes. For Haynes Peleus is emerging from a rustic shrine escorted by Eros and helped by a sea goddess, either Thetis' mother, Dorys, or grandmother Tethys, and watched over by Thetis' father or grandfather, Nereus or Oceanus (cover). Thetis, the object of Peleus' gaze, reclines on the other side of the vase (Pl. 9) attended by Aphrodite, the goddess of love, and her husband, Ares. Others, agreeing that side 'a' shows the wooing of Thetis by Peleus, identify the sea goddess as Thetis and propose alternative explanations for side 'b'. One authority[4] suggests that it shows the wedding of Achilles, Thetis' son, with Helen of Troy on the White Isle after her death watched over by Aphrodite. A recent view[5] suggests that this second side illustrates an episode in Virgil's *Aeneid* when Aeneas, the Trojan hero, encountered Dido, the Carthaginian queen, in a hillside grove above Carthage where they consummated their love watched over by Venus, the goddess of love, or Juno, the goddess of marriage.

Technically the Portland vase is a masterpiece whose manufacture required great skill and long hours of work both for the glass-maker and the glass-cutter who carved the design. It was therefore probably made as a commission for some special occasion. Once thought to have been a funerary urn for the ashes of a

113

Roman emperor, it now seems more likely in view of current interpretation of the
scenes that it was made for a wedding.

The early history of the vase is most obscure.[6] It is supposed to have been found
in 1582 in a tomb occupying the hill on the outskirts of Rome called the Monte del
Grano and to have been associated with the marble sarcophagus in that tomb.
However, this story only dates back to 1697 when it appeared in Pietro Santi
Bartoli's *Gli Antichi Sepolchri*.[7] The earliest trace of the vase is the winter of
1600–1 when it was seen by the Provençal scholar de Peiresc at the Palazzo
Madama.[8] Its owner, the Cardinal del Monte, may have purchased it in 1582, and

scenes on it were shown in drawings from the collection of Cassiano dal Pozzo executed no later than 1590 and possibly much earlier.[9] Drawings of the vase from the same collection (Fig. 86) date from the second decade of the seventeenth century. Its ownership from the time of its sale by the Cardinal is quite easily traceable. It changed hands on the Cardinal's death in 1627 for the sum of 600 *scudi*, becoming the prized possession of Cardinal Francesco Barberini, and was published nine years later by Girolami Teti in *Aedes Barberini*.[10] It remained in the Barberini family until 1780 when it was sold to pay the gambling debts of the Princess of Palestrina, Donna Cornelia Barberini Colonna.

The vase was purchased by James Byres, a Scot, sometime architect turned *cicerone*, or guide, to English and other travellers in Rome and occasional art-dealer. He owned it between 1780 and 1783 and may well have been the first to make any suggestion about how it was made,[11] although de Peiresc knew it was a glass vessel.[12] Within a short time it changed hands yet again, for Byres sold it in early 1783 to Sir William Hamilton, Envoy to the Court of Naples, whose name is forever associated with the bewitching Emma Lyon who arrived in Rome in 1786. Before selling it Byres commissioned sixty plaster casts of the vase to be made by James Tassie from a cast taken by Giovanni Pichler, the gem engraver. One of these casts is in the British Museum collection.[13] Although Hamilton had paid for the vase promptly (he wrote in a letter to Wedgwood that he had paid £1,000 for it), he had been forced to take out a bond on which 5 per cent interest was payable. Soon he too sold the vase, probably because of financial embarrassment, or even perhaps because, like Byres, he enjoyed speculating in antiquities.

In the early summer of 1783 Hamilton returned to England, taking the vase with him. The story of the delicate negotiations leading to the sale of the vase, which were conducted through his niece Mary Hamilton, has been described in detail[14] and need not be retold. By 15 January 1784 the sale of the vase, which the Dowager Duchess of Portland had first seen on 31 December, had been arranged. Originally Hamilton had wanted to sell with the vase a painting then thought to be a Correggio priced at £3,000 so as to raise a total of £4,079, but in the event he appears to have disposed of the vase and three other antiquities for £2,000. Before parting with the vase Hamilton had arranged for it to be drawn by J. B. Cipriani and engraved by Francesco Bartolozzi. It was delivered to Mary Hamilton on Tuesday, 13 July and must have reached the Duchess soon after.

John Flaxman jun., the sculptor (see p. 40), was the first to call the arrival of the vase in England to the attention of Josiah Wedgwood. In a letter from Wardour Street dated 5 February 1784 (E.2-30188) he wrote to Wedgwood:

> I wish you may soon come to town to see Wm Hamilton's Vase, it is the finest production of Art that has been brought to England and seems to be the very apex of perfection to which you are endeavouring to bring your bisque & jasper; it is of the kind called 'Murrina' by Pliny, made of dark blue glass with white enamel figures. The Vase is about a foot high & the figures between 5 & 6 inches, engraved in the same manner as a Cameo & of the grandest & most perfect Greek Sculpture.

Wedgwood replied on 20 February (E.2-30189): 'I am much obliged to you for the information you gave me respecting Sir Wm Hamiltons fine vase, & promise myself an exquisite treat when I do come to town, but the time is at present unavoidably uncertain'.

While the vase was being drawn, prior to its delivery to the Dowager Duchess, it was shown to the Society of Antiquaries of which Hamilton was a leading light, having been a member since 1772. The minutes of the meeting on 11 March read:[15]

> Sir Willm Hamilton was pleased to produce, for the Inspection of the Society a Vase singularly curious brought by him from Italy, and purchased there at a great Expense. It is called, by way of Excellence and Distinction, the *Barbarini Vase* having been many

Years in possession of that Noble Family, and considered by them, and all Travellers of Taste and Judgment, as a Cimelium of extraordinary Curiosity and Value.

The vase's alleged discovery was also reported and it was described as 'formed of a vitrified Composition, of a fine deep transparent blue colour'. Only a few years before it was still thought to have been carved from a hardstone and was referred to in a Roman guide-book of 1750, when in the Library of the Palazzo Barberini, as being 'famosissimo per la qualità della pietra, e suo lavoro'.[16]

The vase, which had aroused such interest, now became part of the Duchess of Portland's renowned private museum. Its presence there must, however, have been a well-guarded secret since Horace Walpole wrote to the Countess of Ossory on 10 August 1785 (not long after the Duchess of Portland's death on 17 July):[17] 'I have heard since my return, that Sir William Hamilton's renowned vase, which had disappeared with so much mystery, is again discovered; not in the tomb, but in the treasury of the Duchess of Portland, in which I fancy it has made ample room for itself. He told me it would never go out of England . . .'. The Duchess of Portland's collection was put up for auction in thirty-eight sessions of over 4,000 lots between 24 April and 7 June 1786. The frontispiece of the sale catalogue (Fig. 87) was an engraving by Charles Grignion after Burney depicting the museum: in a prominent place amongst the seaweeds, medals and books is the vase. Greatly enlarged, it holds a branch of coral and has a mirror behind it to show the reliefs on the reverse side. It was lot 4,155 on the final day of the sale, and in Horace Walpole's opinion was unlikely to produce half of what it cost the Duchess. However, it had not only been discussed in the *Gentleman's Magazine* in February 1785 but also appeared in the Bartolozzi engravings which were published in April 1786, so attention was focused upon it in no small degree.[18]

On 26 April 1786, the third day of the sale but more than a month before the vase was due to be sold, an anonymous article was printed in a London newspaper, the *General Advertiser*. Whoever wrote it may have inspected the vase more closely than would have been possible at the private view held between 12 and 22 April 1786. This is perhaps the only report which does not 'puff' the vase and describes its damaged condition:

This Vase has been broken at least into three pieces, and its original bottom was most certainly destroyed. The present supplemental one (which is connected with all above it by a cincture of enamel yellower than the rest, and serves to hold the fractured parts more firmly together) exhibits a proportion of a figure, which, though female, has been styled an Harpocrates [Egyptian-Roman god of Silence often represented with a finger on his mouth]. It is on a much larger scale than any form on the circumference on the urn, and was evidently an *Appliquée*, though antecedent to the publication of Bartoli, who has described it. This adscititious part is of materials similar to those of which the Vase is composed, though of very different and inferior workmanship; and its edge appears rough from being ground into a circular shape, that it might be accommodated to its present use. It is improbable, however, that any ornament was originally placed where it never could be seen, the vessel itself being designed to rest firmly on a level basis, which must have been rendered unsteady by the projection of any figure embossed on its outside.

At the sale the vase nevertheless produced 980 guineas (£1,029). It was bought by Charles Tomlinson acting for the Third Duke of Portland, son of the late owner, although it had been widely expected to go to the Duke of Marlborough. It is possible that Sir Joshua Reynolds advised the Duke of Portland to buy it.[19] Only three days later Josiah Wedgwood took it on loan with the express purpose of copying it. A receipt for the vase dated 10 June 1786, signed by Wedgwood and witnessed by Thomas Byerley, still belongs to the Wedgwood Museum.[20]

Within two weeks Wedgwood wrote an extremely long letter to Sir William Hamilton. In this letter of 24 June 1786 (E.26-18976) we can almost picture him thinking aloud as he asks for 'advice & directions in several particulars'. Since examining the vase closely he had become aware of the difficulty of copying it,

Figure 87 Frontispiece to Duchess of Portland's sale catalogue 1786, showing the 'Portland Museum', with a fanciful representation of the vase, engraved by Charles Grignion after Burney.

although when working from the engravings in de Montfaucon's *L'Antiquité Expliquée*, issued at Paris in 1722, he had been quite confident of equalling or even excelling the original. It is impossible to know just when Wedgwood decided to copy the classical vase, but it seems quite likely that the idea occurred to him as a result of Flaxman's letter of February 1784. However, although much crestfallen after he had seen the original, he knew he had one advantage over the creators of the glass vase, for his material was much harder, 'nearly as hard as agate . . . & like the agate, it will bear to be cut, and take a polish, at the steel-engraver's lathe. It has likewise a property peculiar to itself, which fits it perfectly for this imitation, which is its taking a blue tint from cobalt, to any degree of strength'. The material was Josiah Wedgwood's jasper ware, the composition of which he was so proud.

Josiah was extremely worried at the outset that he would be unable to find modellers skilled enough to reproduce the reliefs on the vase, or that were he to find them he would be able to pay them properly. Henry Webber (1754–1826), the son of a Swiss sculptor, and the factory's chief modeller, William Hackwood, were to be concerned with the project for three years or so. Webber, previously thought to have been taken on by Wedgwood in 1784 on the recommendation of Sir William Chambers and Sir Joshua Reynolds, is now known to have been associated with the firm some two years earlier.[21] Recently discovered documentary evidence shows that on 8 May 1782 Webber 'agreed with Mr W to go to Etruria'.[22] Between 30 June 1782 and 30 June 1784 he was employed by Wedgwood at £12 12s a month.[23] A formal agreement drawn up on 1 January 1785 specified that he was to be paid the considerable sum of £250 per annum. He was sent to Rome by Wedgwood in July 1787 to make 'Models, Drawings and other Improvements in the Arts of Modelling and Designing'.[24] His stay in Rome lasted until November 1789 when he travelled home with Josiah's eldest son, John, who had also been in Rome. Webber's work in Rome, consisting largely of copying reliefs in the Capitoline Museum and supplying models to the firm,[25] seems to have suited him well. He worked for the potter until Josiah died in 1795 when he began the monument to David Garrick in Westminster Abbey. Wedgwood's doubts about being able to reproduce the figures on the Portland Vase were to be proved unfounded with two such able modellers at his disposal.

The question of the shape of the vase raised some apprehensions in Wedgwood's mind. He thought it 'not so elegant as it might be' but presumed there was some technical reason for this. He contemplated changing the shape but decided against it and consulted Hamilton about whether to copy the reliefs on to alternative shapes and perhaps even add borders or other ornaments. Hamilton does not seem to have positively advised against this. Wedgwood certainly had Pacetti model subjects for plaques taken from the exterior of the sarcophagus in which the vase was supposedly found.

Josiah's commercial instinct was clearly at work at this early stage. He included in the letter previously mentioned a long list of ways in which the vase could be reproduced:

> The working artist would be content with a true & simple copy, a cast in one colour, of a durable material, with the price accordingly. Others, who could afford to proceed a step farther, would desire the addition of a blue ground, though painted only; and a third class would wish to have this addition in the composition of which the vase itself is made, & equally permanent, a fourth perhaps would pay for polishing this durable blue ground, and these two last would be my customers for Jasper copies.

Towards the end of the letter Wedgwood asked Hamilton some very specific questions: should he copy even the parts of the reliefs where mistakes appeared to have been made, should he restore the original smoothness of the reliefs, or 'let the copies pass deficient as time has left the original', and should he use the reliefs for seals, cameos and plaques? In the last part of the letter we come to the formulation of the sales plan which Wedgwood was to follow:

> Several gentlemen have urged me to make my copies of the vase by subscription, and have honored [sic] me with their names for that purpose; but I tell them, & with great truth, that I am extremely diffident of my ability to perform the task they kindly impose upon me; and that they shall be perfectly at liberty, when they see the copies, to take or refuse them; and on these terms I accept of subscriptions, chiefly to regulate the time of delivering out the copies, in rotation, according to the dates on which they honor me with their names.

This may well be the first ever limited edition of a ceramic item intended for sale. Hamilton replied on 24 July[25a] in a somewhat extravagant style:

> It gives me much satisfaction to find that the Barberini Vase not only remains in England, but is in your hands, as I well know that no one can make a better use of it . . . Except the Apollo Belvedere, the Niobes, and two or three others of the first-class marbles, I do not

believe that there are any monuments of antiquity existing that were executed by so great an artist . . . You have seen so well into the difficulties you will have to encounter if you attempt an exact copy of this vase, that I have really nothing to add to the reflections you have made on the subject, and I much approve of your beginning with the most simple copies; and I much approve likewise of your making copies of single figures, and even of the heads; in short, you cannot multiply this wonderful performance too much, but I am convinced, as you say, that an exact copy of the vase, finished by the engraver, would be too expensive to find a purchaser in Europe . . . You are very right in there being some little defects in the drawing; it would, however, be dangerous to touch that, but I should highly approve of your restoring in your copies what has been damaged by the hands of time . . . I should have thought my friend Flaxman would have been of use to you in your present undertaking; for I must do him the justice to say, I never saw a bas-relief executed in the true simple antique style half so well as that he did of the Apotheosis of Homer from one of my vases. If you could instead of sky blue, make your ground look like an onyx, as in the vase itself, it would be better, for there is no natural stone of the sky-blue colour. Unless you hold up the Barberini Vase to the light, it appears to be of a real onyx, and was long mistaken for one . . . I think with you the form might be more elegant, and I would try one more elegant, but it must be simple.

For four years Josiah, his son Josiah II, Webber, Hackwood and others struggled to reproduce the vase. Wax models were made from which working moulds were taken, and a long series of trials were executed. Evidence of this painstaking work survives in the Wedgwood Museum, giving a good idea of the difficulty of the task.

Some idea of the problems encountered in firing the vase can be gained from a letter of 24 March 1788 (W/M 1460) from Josiah II to his father: 'The Barberini vase I mentioned is come out [of the kiln] this morning but the shoulder was turned too thin & it is sunk in – The darker one will go in sometime next week.' A draft letter dated 16 June 1787 (E.26-19090) from Josiah I to Sir William Hamilton written at the time John Flaxman was preparing to depart for Italy (he left in early 1788) thanks him for his 'obliging letter of 25th May'. During a discussion of the projects he has in hand he writes:

But my great work is the Portland vase. I have now finished a third & last edition of the figures *the two first being suppressed in hopes of making the third the more perfect, in this I have certainly succeeded but how far I have done is upon the whole* [the section between * and * is inserted above the line] with what success others must determine. My present difficulty is to give those beautiful shades to the thin & distant parts of the figures, for which the original artist availed himself of the semitransparency of the white glass, cutting it down nearer and nearer to the blue ground, in proportion as he wished to increase the depth of shade. But the case is very different with me. I must depend upon an agent, whose effects are neither at my command, nor to be perceived at the time they are produced, viz. the action of fire on my compositions: a little more or a little less fire, and even the length of time employed in producing the same degree, will make a very material difference in this delicate operation. I am now engaged in a course of experiments for determining these points with as much precision as the nature of the case will admit of, and this is now the only thing that retards the completion of this grand object.

More than two years later, on 9 May 1790, after he had made at least one successful vase, Wedgwood wrote a long letter (E.26-18993) to his son from the showroom at Greek Street, Soho, revealing his energy, method and persistence:

2 trials of Barberini black. With respect to color, they are very much alike, & both very nearly the same as the vase I have with me. But in another respect, the total absence of cracks on the surface, that made of an equal mixture of blue & black, & then dipt in black, has the preference very greatly. It is indeed entirely free from cracks, which the other is not: & as it seems to agree perfectly with both your whites, the yellow & the blue white, I would have you proceed with that in order to lose no time, & be getting more raw materials prepared. I think Dan Hollinshead & his brother should be kept entirely on the vase. For I have 20 copies subscribed for now, but this is only for yourselves, & must not be mentioned at the works for obvious reasons, I mean, that you should not mention its being greatly approved of, or many copies subscribed for – only let them go gently & steadily on with that as with any other work. But though I would have you going on with this composition which we know will do, I wish you at the same time to be making trials with the blue clay, to make it take a black dip without cracking; perhaps a little 59,

or some ball clay, may have that good effect. The cracks are exceedingly minute, not visible when dry, even with a magnifying glass, but when the piece is wetted, they become distinguishable just before it is quite dry, by their deeper colour, the cracks retaining the water longer than the sound part of the surface.

I wish you to look at the left leg of Pluto between the calf and the ancle [sic] the latter of which is not seen, & compare it with a cast out of the mould taken from the vase itself which you will find in one of the drawers of the cabinet closet, this part is said to be too broad. If so, it must be narrowed a little.

Another deficient part in the vase I have is rather owing to accident, from the extreme thinness of the part, I mean the ham and upper part of the calf of the figure entering into Elysium, being jagged.

Some of the vases may be made with the white without any blue in it, & some with the yellow white, as I know that diff.t people will have different tastes.

The theory I proceed upon with respect to cracking is this, that the black diminishes more in burning than the blue, and therefore must crack if it keeps applied to the blue in every part. As 59 mixed with the blue will cause it to diminish in burning proportionably to its quantity, to a certain degree, there is a proportion which will make it diminish exactly the same with the black; that proportion is to be found out, & the cracking is cured. I congratulate you on the success you have had in making one body, the mixture of blue & black, perfect in this respect . . .

During this period of intense experimentation Wedgwood also busied himself with an attempt at discovering the history and significance of the vase. A printed *Account of the Barberini, now the Portland, Vase,* which is in the Library of the Department of Medieval and Later Antiquities, is inscribed on the flyleaf in ink 'From the Author [probably in Josiah's hand]. Received as a present from/M.r Wedgewood [sic] April 28.th 1788.' Facing page 1 is printed:

Mr. Wedgwood is endeavouring to collect all the accounts of the Barberini [crossed out in ink and 'Portland' substituted above] vase that have hitherto been published. He takes the liberty of submitting to his friends the present state of his collection; and will be very thankful for any further information they may be pleased to give him, or any other books they may direct him to in which this subject is mentioned [continues in manuscript, probably in Josiah's own hand]; that the account which he means to deliver with his copies of the vase, may be as complete as possible.

Wedgwood's printed account, which is forty-three pages long, must have taken some time to prepare and was clearly intended to increase the desirability of his product.

The first to receive a perfect copy of the vase was Erasmus Darwin. On 28 June 1789 (E.26-19001) Wedgwood wrote an interesting letter to Darwin, his friend and the family doctor, outlining his method: '. . . first I only pretend to have attempted to copy the fine antique forms, but not with absolute servility. I have endeavoured to preserve the stile & sp.t or if you please the elegant simplicity of the antique forms, & so doing to introduce all the variety I was able, & this Sir W. Hamilton assures me I may venture to do, & that it is the true way of copying the antique.' It was sent to him in September 1789 together with a warning not to show it to anyone outside his own family. However, Darwin could not resist the temptation, as we see from a letter he wrote to Wedgwood:[26] 'I have disobeyed you and shown your vase to two or three; but they were philosophers, not cogniscenti. How can I possess a jewel, and not communicate the pleasure to a few Derby philosophers?' The vase had already been the subject of correspondence between Darwin and Wedgwood in July. Darwin was in the course of writing his long poem *The Botanic Garden,* the second part of which was published in 1791, and included in it a description of the figures on the vase. Wedgwood had urged him (E.26-19002) to see 'the cameo of all cameos . . . the late Barberini, now Portland vase'. He continued: 'The various explications of the bas reliefs upon this famous work of antiquity which I have collected, & think you have a copy of, might furnish even a minor poet with subjects for a few lines; what effect must it have then on a fancy & genius of the first order.'

Darwin's interpretation of the scenes on the vase is highly symbolical. For him

The Portland Vase

Figure 88 Engraving by William Blake illustrating 'Note XXII. – Portland Vase' in Erasmus Darwin's *The Botanic Garden*, part 1, London, 1791. Copyright British Library.

the vase is a 'mystic urn' depicting man's passage from life to death. From a letter written to him by Wedgwood on 17 November 1789 (E.26-19000) it is clear that Darwin had asked to use engravings of the vase to illustrate his poem, to which Wedgwood took no exception. However, he was slightly worried in case the use of any of the prints by Bartolozzi after Cipriani might infringe the copyright belonging to Sir William Hamilton. All these problems must have been resolved, but the engravings Darwin finally used have been attributed to William Blake (Fig. 88).[27] On 23 July 1791 J. Johnson, the publisher, wrote to Darwin: 'Blake is certainly capable of making an exact copy of the vase, I believe more so than Mr B[artolozzi], if the vase were lent him for that purpose, and I see no other way of its being done, for the drawing he had was very imperfect . . .'.[28] Blake probably had access to the vase in the autumn of 1791.

Once the manufacture of the vase was under way and Wedgwood knew that he was able to reproduce the original to his satisfaction, he began to put in hand marketing arrangements. Just as he had displayed the service made for the Empress Catherine in his London showrooms before its dispatch to Russia, so he put on public exhibition in his Greek Street, Soho, showroom in April and May 1790 an example of the Portland Vase. One of the engraved admission tickets, of which 1,900 were printed, is reproduced in Fig. 89. He also ensured that the vase captured the attention of influential men of taste by giving a private showing of it at Sir Joseph Banks's house in Soho Square. The event is recorded in the *General Evening Post*, issued between Saturday, 1 May and Tuesday, 4 May 1790, and the *Gazetteer and New Daily Advertiser*, of Wednesday, 5 May:[29]

> On Saturday night last there was a numerous *converzationi* at Sir Joseph Banks's, Soho-square, when Mr Wedgwood produced the *great vase*, manufactured by himself, in imitation of that superb one about four years ago exhibited in the Museum of her Grace the Duchess Dowager of Portland. The vase is as large as the original; the ground colour that of an emerald, embossed with white. It is most exquisitely finished, and allowed by all present *in point of look*, to be at least equal to the original, which was valued at *two thousand five hundred pounds*.

> The whole of the above vase is a composition of the most beautiful transparency, and does infinite credit to the artist. He has not yet, however, arrived at the *certainty* of *casting* them, as several cracked in the experiment.

> Beside Sir Joseph and a numerous company who attended on the above occasion, there were present Sir Joshua Reynolds, Mr Locke, the Hon. Horace Walpole and several members of the Royal and Antiquarian Societies.

Figure 89 Engraved admission ticket to view the Portland Vase, April and May 1790, at Greek Street, Soho. 9 cm (3½ in) × 6.4 cm (2½ in). Courtesy Josiah Wedgwood and Sons Ltd.

Queen Charlotte, who had requested to see the classical vase when it was in Hamilton's possession, desired to see Wedgwood's copy. Her Majesty had patronised the potter since 1765 when he supplied her with creamware, and she continued to take an interest in his productions. She seems to have made an arrangement to see the vase in early May 1790. M. de Luc, the Queen's personal secretary, wrote to Wedgwood on 5 May apologising for not being present when the Queen saw the vase and requesting to see it himself at some future date.[30] To royal approval was added the cachet of a certificate signed by Sir Joshua Reynolds, President of the Royal Academy. The document was dated 15 June 1790 (now missing) and read: 'I can venture to declare it a correct and faithful imitation both in regard to general effect, and the most minute detail of the parts.'

By June preparations for a promotional tour around the major capitals of Europe by Thomas Byerley and Josiah Wedgwood II were already under way. They left England at the end of June, and on 2 July the young Josiah wrote to his father from Rotterdam to inform them of their safe arrival on foreign shores.[31] They continued immediately to The Hague where the vase was shown to Lord Auckland, then English Ambassador to the Dutch court. Auckland had been a correspondent and customer of Wedgwood's for some years and was more than accommodating in making arrangements for the vase to be shown to the Princess of Orange and to 'the first people that are at the Hague'.

The Princess Wilhelmina was suitably impressed by the occasion writing to her son the next day (6 July):[32]

> Hier nous avons eu un grand déjeuné chez l'Ambassadeur d'Angleterre. Le but de cette fête étoit de voir les échantillons de la manufacture de Wedgwood que le fils de celui qui en est l'inventeur et d'après lequel la fabrique porte le nom, a porté ici et qu'il va montrer dans les principales villes d'Allemagne, afin de faire voir les progrès de la fabrique et établir des correspondances nouvelles. L'associé de son père étoit aussi avec lui. Ils avoient des choses charmantes; et la plus belle, la principale, sur laquelle toute l'attention devoit tomber, étant considérée comme le chef d'oeuvre de l'art, étoit un vase imité de l'antique d'après celui que le duc de Portland possède dans son cabinet et qui est connu sous le nom de *Vase Barberini*, parce qu'il fut trouvé le siècle passé sur une petite hauteur près de Rome pendant le pontificat d'Urbain VIII, de la famille de Barberini. C'est un morceau superbe et dont il n'existe que cette seule copie, qui est parfaitement bien rendue à ce que disent les connoisseurs.

[Yesterday we attended a grand luncheon at the English ambassador's. The aim of the entertainment was to see samples from the Wedgwood factory, brought hither by the son of their inventor after whom the factory is named, which are going to be shown in the main towns in Germany so as to demonstrate the progress made by the factory and to establish new contacts. His father's associate was also with him. They had some charming things, and the most beautiful, indeed, the principal object on which everyone's attention was directed, since it is considered as a masterpiece of the art, was a vase copied from the Antique after one in the Cabinet of the Duke of Portland which is known as the Barberini Vase because it was found in the last century on a little hill near Rome during the pontificate of the Barberini Pope Urban VIII. It is a superb piece and is unique, having been perfectly preserved according to the connoisseurs.]

Although the Princess bought bracelets, she did not, however, subscribe to the vase as had been hoped. Josiah confessed in a letter of 13 July (W/M 1529) to Byerley that he was nevertheless pleased with his son's account of the occasion. He came straight to the point in the first paragraph of his letter: 'I shall be glad to know when you write next whether you think the price of the Barberini vase was any reason why you had no subscribers; & whether Ld. Auckland took any notice of the price.' For Byerley's edification Josiah enclosed a list of the company, eighty people in all, who attended the breakfast, as well as a copy of Lord Auckland's letter to him describing the occasion and praising the young Josiah.

The party travelled to Frankfurt, Berlin, The Hague and Hanover, at times depositing the vase in suitable high-class shops run by business connections of the Wedgwood firm. Here it could be examined by the nobility and 'first people'. This procedure was followed in Amsterdam and Frankfurt.

Wedgwood was still unsure about the price he should charge for the vase, which was 50 guineas at this time, although it was later to drop to 30 for perfect copies which were supplied with a case costing £2 10s. In a letter postmarked 14 September (W/M 1529) addressed to the young Josiah in Frankfurt he expresses his anxieties:

> With respect to the Barberini Vase I do not yet know what to say about the price. I have not yet been able to make another good one. I have fired five more since you left us, & not one near so good as that you have, nor indeed fit to shew; so that unless we are more successful, 50L is too little to save us from loss. Perhaps it would not be amiss to say this to some of the Nobless – however, there is no appearance at present of its being at all prudent to fix the price at less than 50 . . .

Josiah firmly told his son not to part with the vase he had taken with him but to bring it back to Etruria, which he duly did in December. By that time Josiah had realised that the very renown of the vase had made it liable to plagiarism. In a letter of 12 December 1790 (W/M 1529) welcoming Byerley back he explains how his competitors, notably Neale, were cashing in on his success:

> Another disagreeable thing which has lately come to my knowledge is a plaster man, a journeyman to somebody in London or Birm.m I know not which, keeps a room in the pottery [i.e. of his rival] & engages to furnish them with casts of any thing I make. One channel by which he is enabled to perform this is, the Mounters of cameos, who suffer casts to be taken from those they have in their hands for a trifle. And you know that one of our people who was in our warehouse some time ago furnish'd a man of this sort in Oxford road or Holborn with casts from our own bas reliefs. Whether we have any of that description now, a porter, cleaner of ware &c. you will do well to endeavor to find out . . . He engages to furnish the potters with casts from any one of our bas reliefs or cameos they will name – of the Barberini vase as soon as it appears for sale . . .

Sir William Hamilton did not see Wedgwood's copy of the vase until the following summer. A letter addressed to 'Mr Wedgwood' at 'No 4 York Buildings Weymouth' from his son bearing the postmark 20 July 1791 (W/M 1460) contains the following brief report: 'Sr W. Hamilton was here on Satt.y and would have staid a day or two if you had been at home; He was very much pleased with the Barberini Vase.'

Shortly after visiting Etruria Hamilton himself wrote to Wedgwood from Newcastle under Lyme on 23 July 1791 (E.30-22498):

Sir –

Not having had the good fortune to meet with you in London I determined to take Etruria on my way to Derbyshire where I am going to make a visit. I am now just returned from your house, & much disappointed at not having had the pleasure of finding either you or my Naples acquaintance at home. However I have accomplished one of my great objects which was the seeing your wonderful Copy of the Portland Vase. I that am so well acquainted with the Original and the difficulties you must have met with, realy [sic] think it so. The sublime character of the Original is wonderfully preserved in your Copy & little more is wanting than the sort of transparency which your materials could not imitate, to induce those not quite so knowing as you and I are, to mistake it for the Original, in short I am wonderfully pleased with it, and give you the greatest credit for having arrived so near the imitation of what I believe to be the first specimen of the excellence of the Arts of the Ancients existing . . .

There has been a great deal of debate about exactly how many Portland Vases were produced for this first edition. A page apparently from a notebook compiled by Byerley in 1789 lists potential purchasers,[33] but many, such as the Prince of Wales, who later ordered several, did not actually buy. The 'Oven Book', or record of kiln firings, which may be incomplete, documents forty-five copies, which are probably all that were made for the first edition. Of these ten were broken, and doubtless not all the unbroken ones came out of the kiln perfect. Many attempts have been made to trace the original first copies, which are said always to have a pencilled number inside the lip, the significance of which is still unclear, but it has proved well-nigh impossible to discover exactly who bought them. Amongst the clients who certainly bought and paid for Portland Vases are: Thomas Hope, collector, connoisseur and merchant of Amsterdam, 1793; Duke of Marlborough, received 1797, paid 1799; John Sneyd, received 1797, paid 1801; Earl of Mansfield; Edward Constable; Sir James Pulteney; Lord Viscount Lismore; Duchess of Wurtemberg; Dr T. Beddoes; Dr Erasmus Darwin; and Dr R. W. Darwin. The French Republic received a vase in 1802, and a receipt for it from Chaptal is preserved at Keele University,[34] but of the vase there is no trace.

The British Museum has two early jasper copies of the vase, one mid-blue in colour (front cover). This was presented in 1802 by John Wedgwood, Josiah's eldest son. It was one of the earliest pieces of contemporary pottery in the Museum, which generally confined itself to collecting historical, archaeological and ethnographical material. The blue Portland is lighter in weight than the black example and somewhat smaller in height. It has suffered in the firing and is noticeably warped all around the lower part of the body. The sea goddess's left foot has been almost completely lost, quite probably at the time of firing, although the chip to the right arm of the male figure (Ares) at the right may be more recent. Otherwise the vase is undamaged and the leaves are remarkably preserved, in contrast to those on the black version which were too thin, particularly on the side showing Peleus. The disc on the base also has thicker reliefs than on the black vase, but there is a tiny chip to its edge and the small finger of the figure is missing.

The other vase, the surface of which is a rather dull black with no trace of blue (Pl. 9), has a pencilled 'n⁰ 4' inside the lip and is of superior quality, although not entirely without defects. In places, such as on the foliage, the reliefs are too thin so that the black shows through, and there are signs of slight over-firing. These include a small bubble at the base of the right-hand part of the column or 'rustic shrine' from which Peleus emerges and several bubbles on the foliage of the base disc. There is another bubble beside Ares' left heel on the other side of the vase (he is the figure at the right of the scene). Part of the foliage has become detached above the cap worn by the figure on the base, and the base disc is marked with pinholes, as on the blue example and on many other Portland Vases examined by the author. As these pinholes tend to be around the edge of the disc in almost every case, there is the possibility that the vase was fired in the upright position being held by some sort of circular support, perhaps dusted with sand to prevent it adhering to the vase. Finally, the reliefs on the black vase have a rather 'chalky' appearance and are considerably more yellow in tone than those on the blue example. The vase belonged to Mr Isaac Falcke at least as early as 1856 when it was exhibited in the Ceramic Court at the Crystal Palace.

Despite the rarity of the Wedgwood first-edition Portland Vases, many public collections in Britain boast at least one copy. Examples can be seen in Liverpool, Port Sunlight, Nottingham, Edinburgh, Barlaston (the Wedgwood factory museum) and London. Some vases have been sold to collectors in the United States, and others are in museums there, notably in Boston, Massachusetts, and Chicago, Illinois. There is still a strong market for early copies of the vase, one being sold in London in 1981 for £27,000.[35]

The story of the Portland Vase did not end with Josiah Wedgwood's first edition, which it can be guessed was more of a prestige production than a profit-making venture. There have been subsequent editions made at the factory, the most recent being of blue jasper ware made in 1980 for the 250th anniversary of Josiah's birth. It has been said by certain writers that vases were made in the early nineteenth century, but as there were a number of the original edition still unsold in the warehouse in 1828 (ten were sold to the glassmaker Apsley Pellatt in 1829),[36] it seems highly unlikely that any more were produced until the edition of 1839 which had the peculiar distinction of having the figures remodelled to include drapery as a gesture to Victorian prudery.[37]

Copies of the vase have been produced in some quantity in various sizes and colours at the factory from the late nineteenth century until the late 1930s and are by no means rare. The late vases lack the exquisite finish of the pieces made under Josiah's supervision and can usually be easily distinguished from an early copy without even a direct visual comparison being necessary. An interesting document casts a little more light on the matter of the various types of vase made, both at the factory and elsewhere. A receipt preserved amongst the Wedgwood papers and dated 18 February 1878 (E.33-32896) reads: 'Received from Mr Joseph Holdcroft of London the sum of fifty pounds for *an "old" seconds original Portland Vase* for many years in the possession of the late Mr Aaron Wedgwood carver and gilder Burslem. The said Vase was lent to Messrs Boote of Burslem to execute their *"prize vase"* for *The Exhibition in 1851*.' T. and R. Boote of Burslem bought the Waterloo works in 1850, according to W. Chaffers,[38] and patented improvements in tile making. The firm participated in the 1851 Exhibition. It is interesting to note that the 'seconds' of the vase were kept for so many years and were considered so valuable in 1878. The popularity of the Portland Vase, which has continued up to the present day, seems to have justified the painstaking work put in by Josiah for so little financial reward.

Figure 90 Creamware vase or
column intended for a clock,
decorated with buff-coloured
slip, unmarked, perhaps
c. 1809. Diam. 7⅛ in (18 cm).
H. 12¼ in (31 cm). Presented by
Mr and Mrs Isaac Falcke,
1909.

7 Nineteenth- and twentieth-century Wedgwood

After Josiah Wedgwood's death in 1795 the management of the enterprise he had founded passed to his son Josiah II and his nephew Thomas Byerley. Byerley had long been responsible for the London showroom and was soon also in charge of the Etruria factory. Located at Portland House in Greek Street, Soho, between 1774 and 1795 (a blue plaque supplied by the company marks the premises),[1] the showroom then moved to the corner of York Street (now Duke of York's Street) and St James's Square. A coloured engraving from Ackermann's *Repository of Arts* of 1809[2] shows a view of the premises which were stocked with a wide variety of items, including pillars or fluted columns resembling a creamware example in the British Museum collection decorated with buff slip (Fig. 90). Although long called a vase, there is a possibility that the object may have been designed as part of a clock. A Royal Inventory records that a somewhat similar column, of Sèvres manufacture, once held a movement by the French maker Dutertre. The movement is still in the Royal Collection.[3] Another mantel clock, dating from about 1780, the dial signed by Dubois of Paris, incorporates a fluted porcelain column, from an unidentified factory, to which the dial is attached.[4] However, the purpose of this Wedgwood column is still a matter for debate, as no clocks incorporating them are known. We do know, however, that such columns were still on sale in the early nineteenth century and were in the Wedgwood factory pattern book still in use in 1920.

A large marble clock (Fig. 91) was in fact delivered to its original owner on 9 October 1799. With its two recumbent bronze sphinxes cast and chased by Hoole, supporting the dial and perched on a rectangular block of marble, the whole surmounted by a swooping gilt-bronze eagle, it exhibits a mixture of styles. Sphinxes in the Egyptian taste, which became increasingly popular from the mid-1770s, have been combined with a neoclassical eagle, whilst the relief on the jasper plaque alludes only distantly to its classical prototypes. This clock is one of the few pieces incorporating a Wedgwood plaque which is securely datable from a document. An extract from the workbook of the clockmaker Benjamin Vulliamy (1747–1811), one of the leading makers of his day, gives us every detail concerning its assembly:[5]

308.	Marble Clock with 2 Bronze Sphinxes	
	Day the Marble	5– 8– 0
	Bullock the Mov^t	5– 0– 0
	Long & Drew the dial plate	14– 0
	Culver engraving the hands	5– 6
	Crockett the gilding	1–16– 0
	Two sphinxes by Hoole, casting & chasing	3–10– 0
	Amidroz engraving the two plates	1– 0– 0
	Hoole for a small rosette	– – –
	Wedgwood the Medallion	1– 1– 0

Huguenin the brass work 8 days	2– 0– 0
Haas the brass ring	2– 6
Hoole casting & chasing the eagle	2–10– 0
Crockett gilding the eagle	2– 5– 0
Oswald the oval stand	– – –
Desperrin the glass shade	1–11– 6

Del[d] to R. Borough Esq. Oct[r] 9 1799.

The oval plaque of Bacchanalian boys at play was designed by Lady Diana Beauclerk (see p. 59) between 1783 and 1787. Although it is possible that the plaque was taken from stock, it is just as likely that Mr Borough ordered it specially, even though the order has not yet been discovered. The incorporation of Wedgwood plaques and medallions into furniture, candelabra and clocks was particularly popular in France from the late eighteenth century onwards, with contemporary French documents often even containing mistaken information regarding the origin of similar French-made plaques recorded as being English, and vice versa. The Vulliamy clock is an example of the practice of mounting plaques in this way in England for an English customer.[6]

When Thomas Byerley died in September 1810, he had completed over thirty years of service with the Wedgwood firm. He had certainly helped to maintain continuity after the death of Josiah I, whose sons, by virtue of the easy circumstances of their upbringing, were very different from their father. The eldest, John (1766–1844), seems to have particularly delighted in living the life of a gentleman.[7] He received a fine liberal education, attended the University of Edinburgh in 1785, and travelled extensively in Europe. Together with his two brothers, and his cousin Thomas Byerley, he had joined the partnership of Wedgwood, Sons and Byerley in January 1790 and remained a partner until 1793. At the same time he became from 1792 a junior partner in the London banking firm of Alexander Davison and Co. In 1800 he rejoined the Wedgwood partnership on the expiry of the original seven-year term. By now his financial affairs were in considerable disarray, and the pottery was being neglected by the second son, Josiah II (1769–1843), at a time when trade in general was adversely affected by the Napoleonic Wars. Josiah II in fact lived in Surrey and then in Dorset between 1795 and 1804, although he was in charge of the works and paid visits to it, returning to Staffordshire permanently in 1804. Between 1800 and 1807 it was John Wedgwood who made the greatest contribution to the affairs of the factory and his influence is traceable both in surviving papers recording his plans and in the pieces themselves.

John Wedgwood instituted a programme of expansion at the factory. He was aided by the installation of a new Boulton and Watt steam-engine, which supplied power from 1796 and was still in use when the great French ceramic chemist Alexandre Brongniart[8] visited Etruria in 1834. The factory was enlarged and a printing-works set up. Blue-printed patterns and new firing methods were introduced, as well as a new range of patterns. Many of them reflected John Wedgwood's deep love and knowledge of horticulture (he was one of the founders and first Treasurer of the Royal Horticultural Society established in 1804) and were closely copied from botanical engravings.

Amongst the most remarkable of all services made during this period is the well-known pearlware 'Water Lily' service ordered in 1807 and delivered in 1808 to Dr Robert Darwin, son of Dr Erasmus Darwin and father of the evolutionist Charles Darwin. A plate from this service (Pl. 14a) was given to A. W. Franks by Dr Joseph Hooker (1817–1911), Director of Kew Gardens between 1865 and 1885 and friend of Charles Darwin. The 'Water Lily' pattern almost certainly represents the earliest use of brown underglaze printing in Staffordshire that can be accurately dated.[9] The decision to introduce the manufacture

Figure 91 Marble clock with bronze sphinxes supplied by Benjamin Vulliamy to R. Borough in October 1799. The blue jasper ware plaque depicts in relief Bacchanalian boys at play designed by Lady Diana Beauclerk, 1783–7. The same scene decorates the wine cooler in Fig. 47. Total H. 18½ in (46.8 cm). H. of plaque 5¾ in (14.7 cm). Presented by Mr and Mrs Isaac Falcke, 1909.

Figure 92 Pearlware plate printed in underglaze-blue with a dock and a bramble, impressed WEDGWOOD ETRURIA, zz, and 11 painted in underglaze-blue, 1840–5. Diam. 8 in (20.4 cm). Presented by Mr and Mrs Isaac Falcke, 1909.

of underglaze printed ware at Etruria (overglaze printing having been used since the 1770s) was taken on 31 March 1805. The 'Water Lily' pattern was the first to be used at Etruria that reproduced identifiable botanical prints. The engravings of the water lilies, all members of the *Nymphaeaceae* family, indigenous to watery places, have been identified as:[10] *nymphaea stellata*, or starry water lily, on the left; *nymphaea lotus*, or Lotus of Egypt, on the right; and *nelumbium speciosum*, or sacred Lotus of Buddha, the fully opened flower in the centre, with large, veined indented leaves. The lilies were all copied either from the *Botanist's Repository* or from the *Botanical Magazine*, periodicals published between October 1803 and February 1806.

A smaller pearlware plate is printed overglaze in orange with this pattern[11] and was probably intended for soup. The brown water-lily design was in production only for a short time between early 1808 and May 1811 when Josiah II commanded that all the 'Brown Lily' in the London showrooms should be turned out, since the design could only be executed at a loss. Instead it was to be printed in blue, a colour which is much more commonly found as it has been kept in production over a long period.

A pearlware dessert plate in the British Museum collection has a looped border motif and two plants in the well of the dish printed in blue. The source of these plants has not yet been discovered (Fig. 92). They are a member of the *Rubus* or bramble family, to judge from the spiny stem, and a *Rumex*, or dock, or possibly a *Polygonum*.[12] The design may have originated in the days of John Wedgwood, but the plants have been printed facing in opposite directions, an example of careless workmanship which he cannot have intended. On the whole John Wedgwood's botanical productions were of high quality. The rare mark (cf. Fig. 96) denotes that this plate was manufactured between 1840 and 1845, a time when the factory reached a rather low ebb in its fortunes. It is likely to have been a replacement for an earlier broken piece, as this type of decoration was out of fashion by the middle of the century.

The earliest years of the nineteenth century were marked not only by the revival of printing, which was being so widely used at other Staffordshire firms, but also by the adventurous use of another type of decoration currently popular, and one which had been investigated, although apparently not put into production during the Wedgwood and Bentley era. Thomas Bentley had carried out experiments in 1776 and recorded the results in the 'London Experiment Book' which show that he had come close to achieving lustre effects. He knew that the principle was to fire metals in an oxygen-starved, or reducing, atmosphere, a technique developed in the Near East in the ninth century and popular in sixteenth-century Italy. In the second decade of the eighteenth century the Saxon porcelain manufacturer Johann Böttger discovered the secret of making a purple lustre. Metallic lustres, that is, painted lustres fired in an oxidising atmosphere, and consisting of metallic compounds combined with resin and oil, were developed in England in the early nineteenth century,[13] and potteries in both Staffordshire and Sunderland made them in some quantity. Thought to have first been used at Spode in November 1805, they are not normally associated with Wedgwood, although some examples from the factory are in the British Museum.

A magnificent shell centrepiece and a cream bowl and cover, spoon and stand (Pl. 14b) are in fact merely thickly gilded, but their decoration resembles metallic lustre. The centrepiece, perhaps used to hold fruits, is of pearlware and is in the form of a shell commonly called the 'Paper Nautilus',[14] reproduced in a highly accurate form but several times its natural size. The shell, of worldwide distribution, was first described by Linnaeus in 1758, and is actually an egg case for an octopod called *Argonauta argo*. It rests on a flesh-toned stand imitating coral. The base is formed as a shell of the *Tellina* family, possibly slightly adapted in order to support the weight of the upper part. The only decoration is lavish gilding on the rim to highlight the 'ribs' of the shell and to outline the form of the *Tellina* shell below. The centrepiece probably once had a matching stand similar in shape to one in the Ford Museum, in Dearborn, Michigan (USA).[15] The cream bowl and cover, with their spoon and stand, are decorated in the same technique. Together the bowl and cover form a brachiopode, probably based on a British fossil, and were perhaps copied direct from specimens found by Josiah I on his fossil-collecting expeditions. The finial has the appearance of a worm tube and is gilded. Like the centrepiece, the tureen rests on a flesh-toned stand, whilst the base closely copies the shell known as the Sunrise Tellin of the genus *Tellina*, found in the Caribbean, but it is more than twice the size of the average shell. The spoon is formed as a slightly stylised scallop-shell of the genus *Pecten*, found in the Caribbean or Indo-Pacific area, and the handle imitates coral. Josiah Wedgwood I was responsible for the original use of these shapes, which have retained their popularity over more than 200 years. In his shape book they are given their correct names, since conchology was one of the potter's great interests during the 1770s (Fig. 93).[16] These pieces have a certain austerity and restraint, which is allied to a most pleasing form, and a rare type of decoration.

Also in the collection are three pieces all decorated with a type of lustre generally referred to as 'variegated' and later referred to erroneously as 'moonlight lustre' (Pl. 14b). Variegated lustre was in production from around 1809.[17] It has a 'marbled' effect of grey achieved using platinum, pink derived from gold, and orange from iron. A small pearlware two-handled ink-well complete with

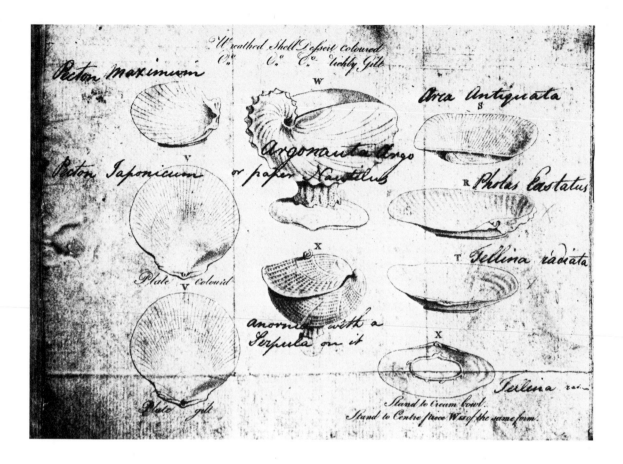

Writhed Shell Dessert coloured
Do Do Do richly Gilt

Pecten maximum

W

Argonauta Argo
or paper Nautilus

Arca Antiquata
S

R Pholas Costatus

Pecten Japonicum
V

Plate Coloured
V

X

anomia with a
Serpula on it

T Tellina radiata

X

Plate gilt

Stand to Cream bowl.
Stand to Centre piece Was of the same form.

Tellina ra...

a diminutive ink container which fits into a well in the centre, itself also detachable, is perhaps the most unusual. The decoration is mottled purple, grey and orange, with a gold-coloured sheen. The lustred base is marked, and has an impressed B. Less rare are pearlware lustred pecten-shell dessert plates, such as the one in the collection bearing the factory mark and an impressed V. The lustres resemble those of the ink-well. Another, slightly larger plate in the British Museum, of the same form and with the same mark, has been decorated not with lustre but in pale pink.[18] The third of the lustred pieces is a jug of a rather deeper pink. The grey is muted, and there are traces left by the feather used to apply the lustres. The rim of the jug is gilded and there are remains of gilding on the sides of the handle.

Manufactured at about the same time is a small group of pieces in a peculiarly English ceramic body called bone china because of the inclusion in it of 50 per cent calcined ox bone. This body, developed (or at least perfected) in 1796 by Josiah Spode,[19] is not normally associated with Wedgwood. It was in fact made by the firm only for a short time in the early nineteenth century, but was re-introduced in 1878 and is now a major part of the firm's output. The first use of bone china at Wedgwood has been traced to the year 1811 when Josiah II embarked on a number of trials.[20] In June 1812 specimens were sent to Josiah Byerley (son of Thomas, and the great-nephew of Josiah I), who was the London business manager. Unfortunately, the samples arrived too late in the season, a mistake that would almost certainly not have been made by Josiah I. However, there proved to be some demand for the ware, especially in the middle years of the second

Figure 93 Page from a Wedgwood pattern book showing shells of various forms for dessert wares with their contemporary identifications. Paper of pattern-book watermarked 1802. For wares of shell form see Pl. 14b. Courtesy Josiah Wedgwood and Sons Ltd.

decade of the nineteenth century. The British Museum has a few pieces intended for domestic use which serve to show how fine this body was and what type of decoration is found on Wedgwood bone china of the first period.

Recent research into pattern names and numbers[21] has shown that there was a considerable number of patterns in production in the early decades of the nineteenth century. They were not only used on bone china but were also suitable for pearlware. A cup and saucer with a printed and painted pattern of butterflies in various tones of brown embellished with gilded decoration (Fig. 94) reflects the prevailing taste for Chinese works of art. So too does the pattern of flowers and bird on a branch painted in delicate colours on a coffee-can, as well as on a cup and saucer (Fig. 95) in the collection. The extremely high quality of the china, almost 'greasy' to the touch, and the clear soft tones of the decoration leave room for regret that so little of it was made.

Botanical subjects, much beloved of the English, also appear on several pearlware plates probably made during the time when John Wedgwood was active in the firm. The most attractive is part of a series depicting botanical flowers rendered with remarkable accuracy in a combination of two different techniques, bat printing (stippling) and hand-colouring (Fig. 96). The green, pink and yellow areas are filled in by hand, and the colouring and the placing of the flowers show a quite exceptional refinement. The larger yellow flower on the right is described in the reverse as 'ochna squarrosa' and was taken from W. Roxburgh's *Plants of Coromandel*, I, 89, published in 1798. The pink flower on the left, 'epigenea repens', was copied from H. Andrews's '*Botanist's Respository*', 2:t 102, which appeared in 1800.[22] The sensitive positioning of the decoration and its careful execution, together with the almost flawless quality of the body, make this piece a minor masterpiece.

Two most unusual earthenware plates (Fig. 97) are also decorated with flowers. Hand-painted, they appear to have been varnished rather than glazed and

Figure 94 Bone china cup and saucer printed in black over the glaze and painted in brown, black, orange and salmon pink with gilt highlights and gilded rims and handle, pattern no. 591 in the Wedgwood pattern book, 'Chinese Butterflies and Sprigs'. WEDGWOOD printed in red on both, 1812–29. H. of cup 2¼ in (5.7 cm). Diam. of saucer 5½ in (14 cm). Presented by A. W. Franks Esq.

resemble *papier mâché*. The rims have traces of gilding. The draughtsmanship is of a sufficiently high standard to have been the work of a professional; however, documents exist which reveal that some pieces at least were requested from the Wedgwood firm by lady artists for decoration at home, a fashion datable to the last years of the eighteenth century.[23]

A vase which is functional, since it has three flower-holders, is a fairly well-known model of hemispherical shape supported on three dolphins and resting on a base of triangular shape (Fig. 98). A number of examples of broadly similar form exist in various different bodies and many of them bear the date 2 February 1805.[24] The significance of this date mark is unknown, despite various theories which have been put forward, none of which seems plausible. It has been suggested that the date commemorates a new partnership or even the development of the lustreing process.[25] Whilst the second theory has been discounted because it is known that John Hancock who worked for Henry Daniel did not perfect the technique until November 1805,[26] the first has never been confirmed from documentary sources. There is the added difficulty that the Wedgwood papers are incomplete for the early years of the nineteenth century. They were apparently disposed of for waste paper and had been partly used as packing material. They were discovered by chance in the early nineteenth century by the Liverpool collector Joseph Mayer (1803–86), who purchased the entire collection. The papers, which were eventually acquired by the Wedgwood family, have often been referred to in this book as being on loan to the University of Keele, North Staffordshire.

The flower-vase, which has a domed lid with a prominent and rather elaborate

Figure 95 (*top left*) Bone china cup and saucer and coffee can printed in grey and painted in pink, blue, orange, yellow and green with pattern 616, 'Chinese bird & flowers in colour & gold border & edge'. WEDGWOOD printed in red on both, 1812–29. H. of coffee can 2⅜ in (6.2 cm). H. of cup 2¼ in (5.8 cm). Diam. of saucer 5⅝ in (14.2 cm). Presented by Mrs Willoughby Hodgson, 1934.

Figure 96 (*bottom left*) Pearlware plate bat printed in brown and hand-coloured with a yellow flower described on reverse as 'ochna squarrosa' (*right*) and a pink flower as 'epigenea repens', pattern no. 492, 'Botanical flowers gold edge', also produced in bone china. In bat printing a plaque of glue covered with oil is used to transfer the design on to the pot. Impressed WEDGWOOD, 7 (twice), *c.* 1815. Diam. 8 in (20.5 cm). Presented by Mr and Mrs Isaac Falcke, 1909.

Figure 98 Unglazed creamware vase and cover with three
flower-holders, decorated with
a band of classical profile heads
within circular medallions in
orange and buff, alternating
with stylised flower motifs on a
black ground, with a floral
wreath and with oak and laurel
leaves on the cover; impressed
WEDGWOOD, late 18th or early
19th century. H. 7⅞ in (20 cm).
Presented by Mr and Mrs
Isaac Falcke, 1909.

knop, is glazed only on the inside. The band of flowers near the neck is noticeably
well executed. The finial to the lid has a detachable stopper which, when removed,
leaves a circular hole presumably to act as another flower-holder. There is the
distinct possibility that it also may have been decorated by an amateur. It is not
easily datable but was probably made and decorated during the first half of the
nineteenth century.

During the late eighteenth and early nineteenth centuries the 'dry body'
known as caneware (see p. 44) seems to have enjoyed some popularity. Its unglazed surface was often decorated with flowers in an Oriental manner. A new
formula for a finer caneware composition was perfected in 1783, and motifs
based on decoration found on eighteenth-century Chinese *famille rose* porcelain
were adapted to please the taste of the European public. The large fish bowl in the

British Museum collection is an exceptional and magnificent example of its kind (Pl. 15a). The shape is also based on a Chinese prototype unlike some of the enamelled basalt wares produced at the Wedgwood factory at this time. The popular Chinese motif of swimming fish which appears inside the bowl and its handles in the form of Chinese dogs' heads show that in this case at least some effort was made towards homogeneity of shape and decoration.

It goes without saying that the other popular unglazed body made at Etruria, jasper ware, continued in production. A tripod pastille burner (Fig. 99), used to perfume rooms or as an ornament, with the dark blue dip so typical of the early nineteenth century, is an example of a category of piece with a mark, already referred to on p. 135, that has never been satisfactorily explained. The British Museum pastille burner lacks its cover, unlike others of the same form in black basalt, 'rosso antico' and lustre which can be found in public and private colections.[27] However, there are two sets of marks on the piece and this is somewhat unusual (Fig. 100). Although the precise date of manufacture of this piece is now a matter of some controversy, there is little doubt that it was made in the early part of the century and gives some idea of the productions of this phase of the factory's existence.

There seems to have been little apparent loss of quality in jasper ware production, despite complaints in correspondence between members of the family concerning the disorder into which the works had fallen. Thomas Byerley made

Figure 99 Dark blue jasper dip pastille burner (cover missing), impressed WEDGWOOD 2 FEB[Y] 1805 and stencilled in grey 'Josiah Wedgwood 2 February 1805'. H. 4½ in (11.6 cm). Presented by Mr and Mrs Isaac Falcke, 1909.

Figure 100 Impressed and stencilled marks on base of dark blue jasper dip pastille burner shown in Fig. 99.

an eloquent comment on the state of business when writing on 1 October 1807 (W/M 1503) from Dublin where he had gone to set up showrooms: '. . . I shod feel more secure if we had something *peculiar*, and in this respect the Jasper may still befriend us, for there is very little of it in the market', but, he added, 'what we have of it is, I fear however more calculated to stand on our shelves & be admired than to produce profit'.

Outstanding pieces, it seems, are sadly lacking during the second and third decades of the nineteenth century and the decoration, such as the painted chrysanthemums found on an oval dish inscribed on the reverse with the pattern number 1157,[28] and on a circular plate,[29] both datable from the pattern number to around 1822, cannot compare with the refinement of a decade earlier. A transfer-printed design in brown of ivy leaves hand-coloured in green found on two pearlware plates[30] is far from the botanical accuracy of some of the pieces mentioned earlier, although the pale custard-yellow border on one is typical of the unusual colours fashionable at this period. Another plate has a most unusual mouse-coloured border (Fig. 101), probably imitating some of the subtle tints found on contemporary English porcelains, which were then beginning to assert their supremacy in world markets.

The firm's failure to maintain the standards set by its founder during the second and third decades of the nineteenth century led to its progressive decline. By 1844 it was in such trouble that the estate, pottery, village and hall were for sale by auction. A printed set of 'Particulars' in the Wedgwood Archive is dated 5 July 1844.[31] The factory did not, as it happened, change hands, as no buyer could be found. At that time the premises were occupied by Messrs Wedgwood and Boyle under a lease which still had five years to run in November 1843. John Boyle had been taken on as a partner to inject capital into the concern, but he lived only until 1845. From the beginning of the partnership established in 1846 with Robert Brown – the association lasted until 1859 – recovery began. However, in the 1820s and 30s little of note was manufactured.

A tea-set, consisting of a teapot and cover, a sugar bowl and cover and a milk jug, dates from the late 1840s (Figs 102, 103). Although red ware used for a new range in 1859[32] has been called 'little better than "kitchen ware" ',[33] the silver mounts and the historic associations attached to these pieces make them

Figure 101 Pearlware plate
decorated with pink star-
shaped flowers with blue veins
and leaves, on a mouse-
coloured ground, blue rim,
impressed WEDGWOOD and
incised workman's marks,
c. 1825. Diam. 8 in (20.5 cm).
Presented by Mr and Mrs
Isaac Falcke, 1909.

worthy of more than just passing attention. The mounts are in the Revived
Rococo style of the 1840s, characterised by the curves and love of asymmetry
associated with the 1750s and 60s. The two covers have carefully worked silver
rosebud finials. The pieces have long been associated with Queen Adelaide
(1792–1849), the wife of William IV. In 1856, not long after the Queen's death,
they belonged to Isaac Falcke, and were exhibited by him at the Crystal Palace
Exhibition. They were mentioned in the *Art Journal* for that year as amongst the
'conspicuous objects exhibited in the Ceramic Court', and their former royal
ownership was alluded to. However, at the time of writing no trace has been found
of this terracotta tea-service in the Royal Archive at Windsor.

The initiative taken by Henry Cole in improving design standards in British
industry, culminating in the Great Exhibition of 1851, had the effect of stimu-
lating the Etruria factory along with other potteries. The factory now entered on
a period of recovery, which was assisted by a revival of jasper ware, which had
begun to interest collectors. Falcke and his generation were among the first to
collect Wedgwood. They admired not only the best contemporary products of the
firm but also early neoclassical pieces from the Wedgwood and Bentley era. This
passion for Wedgwood in all its forms is a strong reflection of the new eclecticism
of the mid-nineteenth century.

A new material, usually known as 'Parian porcelain' but given the name
'Carrara' at Wedgwood, came into production in Staffordshire in the 1840s and
appears to have been used for the first time at Wedgwood in 1847. A type of

WEDGWOOD
ETRURIA

Figure 102 Unglazed red
earthenware teapot and cover,
sugar bowl and cover and milk
jug, mounted in silver, said to
have belonged to Queen
Adelaide (1792–1849). Im-
pressed WEDGWOOD, incised
marks (milk jug), mounts hallmarked London, 1839–40,
maker's mark 1F (James
Franklin?), teapot and milk jug;
WEDGWOOD ETRURIA (sugar
bowl), mount hallmarked
London, 1843, maker's mark
WC (?William Cooper), made
c. 1840–5. H. of teapot and
cover 5¾ in (14.6 cm). Presented by Mr and Mrs Isaac
Falcke, 1909.

Figure 103 Impressed marks
on base of unglazed red
earthenware sugar bowl
(Fig. 102), c. 1840–5.

unglazed soft-paste porcelain, normally used for figures and busts, it was immensely popular in Victorian England. Wedgwood put into production about
140 models, many commissioned from the leading contemporary sculptors.[34]

Although Parian is generally white in colour, some firms including Wedgwood
and Minton, did manufacture tinted Parian. A recently acquired bust of William
Ewart Gladstone (1809–98) is a rare example of green tinted Parian (Fig. 104).
It was made on commission in 1879 for Frederick Rathbone of 71, King's Road,
Brighton, one of the leading Wedgwood dealers of the late nineteenth century,
as an inscription on the reverse of the bust records. The bust was modelled by
Joseph Edgar Boehm (1834–90), a member of the Royal Academy in 1882 and
exhibitor there between 1862 and 1891. Amongst the Gladstone Papers in the
British Library are some letters showing that Boehm requested a sitting with
Gladstone in May 1880, in order to model a bust for Lord Rosebery. Boehm
exhibited a marble bust of Gladstone at the Academy in 1881; but the Wedg-

Figure 104 Parian porcelain
bust of William Ewart
Gladstone (1808–98) by J. E.
Boehm RA (1834–90), tinted
green, made on commission for
Frederick Rathbone, 1879.
Impressed WEDGWOOD
SUBSCRIPTION COPY Frederick
Rathbone, 71 King's Road,
Brighton. Incised J. E. BOEHM·
fecit. 1879.

wood bust clearly antedates this correspondence so it may well not have been
modelled from life.

The production of the bust of Gladstone, which was also made by Wedgwood
for Rathbone in black basalt,[35] was well-timed. Gladstone was in the midst of his
famous 'Midlothian campaign' during the latter part of 1879 and was elected for
a second time as Prime Minister in 1880, displacing Disraeli, whose imperialistic
policies in Afghanistan he had vigorously denounced in the course of his campaign. Numerous drawings depicting Gladstone's triumphant progress in the
Scottish Lowlands appeared in the *Illustrated London News*, showing that he
was the 'man of the moment' in 1879. However, the subscription issue of the
Gladstone bust was a failure, and Rathbone lost money on it. The remainder of
the busts at Etruria around 1900 were sold for a few shillings each.[36] The previous
history of the bust now in the British Museum is unknown – it appeared in a
London saleroom in 1979, exactly 100 years after it was first issued.

Gladstone was a ceramic enthusiast and collector: he had a deep knowledge of English ceramics, the study of which was still in its infancy. In a speech given at the London Institution on 'The History of the Potter's Art in Britain' Gladstone was reported[37] as saying 'Wedgwood is one of the heroes whom I worship'. He recognised, and possibly even overrated, Josiah's contribution towards revolutionising 'the character of the fabrics', and thought he had 'carried the manufacture of earthenware ... to by far the highest point which it has ever attained in any country in the world'. He included in his definition of earthenware anything which was not porcelain – that is, jasper ware, caneware and basalt, as well as creamware. One does rather wonder what he thought of being immortalised in Parian, since he is reported[38] as saying in a speech accepting a Derby china service, 'After Wedgwood and Champion (who made the first hard-paste porcelain produced in these islands) . . . a reign of commonplace set in. A dull and deplorable prettiness occupied the field which reached the last stage of depravity with the invention of "Parian biscuit"'. It is more than likely that Frederick Rathbone never sought Gladstone's approval for the production of his green-tinted Parian bust.

During the high Victorian period the art of painting on ceramics enjoyed a high regard. The 1870s saw the triumph of the English bone china industry, which was competing keenly for foreign markets, especially through the frequent international exhibitions which served as showcases for the most magnificent products of all the leading ceramic factories. Wedgwood participated in these exhibitions, where the work of leading painters aroused considerable admiration. Many of the artists employed in English factories were foreigners, who appear to have been particularly well paid. One of these was Emile Lessore, who had studied with Hersent and the great Ingres in Paris, exhibited at the Paris salons and began painting on ceramics at Bourg-la-Reine (near Paris). He was employed as an artist and designer at the French state porcelain factory at Sèvres before coming to England to work for Minton in about 1858. In 1860 he went to Wedgwood, having briefly worked for the firm on a freelance basis.

Less widely renowned, less well paid, but more typically English in his style of painting was the Minton-trained painter Thomas Allen, who was among the outstanding ceramic artists of the nineteenth century.[39] A native of the Potteries, Allen was one of the first to benefit from the British initiative in setting up art schools for the training of artists in industry: he won a National Art Training Scholarship in 1852 and studied at Somerset House and South Kensington. He became a skilful figure painter, joining Wedgwood from Minton between November 1875 and February 1876. Allen's talent was quickly harnessed, and his work received its first international showing at the Paris Exhibition held in 1878. His pieces were praised in the *Art Journal* for that year, although the signed and dated plaque recently acquired by the British Museum did not actually receive a mention.

The plaque (Pl. 15b), made of creamware of slightly inferior quality, depicts a partly draped Nubian lady in front of a screen flanked on the left side by a massive Egyptian head. On the right are shrubs, probably intended as lemon-trees. The painting displays the subtle eroticism based on the rendering of an exotic and scantily clad female figure which is so often found in Victorian art. Interest in Egyptian civilisation, which provided inspiration for other ceramic factories, was marked at this period, but Allen made no attempt to reproduce accurately the Egyptian motifs he had chosen; he merely used them as decorative elements, interpreting them extremely loosely. Without doubt the plaque represents a notable example of the work of Allen, who was appointed Art Director of the Wedgwood firm in March 1878, a post he held until his partial retirement about twenty

Figure 105 Earthenware pilgrim flask decorated in the sgraffito technique with Egyptian motifs and 'Isis' border in cream, red-brown and black slips and gilded, attributed to Frederick Rhead (1857–1933), c. 1878. The 'Isis' border was also used on the plate decorated by Thomas Allen (see Pl. 15b). Impressed WEDGWOOD, 4 and other illegible marks. H. $11\frac{3}{8}$ in (29 cm).

years later. His influence over the studio and 'art' wares made by Wedgwood was incalculable.

Another recent acquisition is a pilgrim flask with rudimentary handles (Fig. 105), likely to have been executed about 1878 and decorated in a quite different technique, generally known as *sgraffito*, which involves scratching the design through a layer of slip. The theme, however, is the same as that of the Allen plaque, and the Isis border used on both pieces is another indication that the Egyptian style was experiencing a renewed surge of popularity as a source for decorative motifs. The cream and red-brown decoration of an Egyptian head in profile on one side and a scarab on the other has been attributed on stylistic grounds to Frederick Rhead (1857–1933) who was trained in the *pâte-sur-pâte* technique by M. L. Solon at the Minton factory. This method also uses slip, or liquid clay, but it is built up, rather than cut away, to produce a relief effect. Rhead joined Wedgwood in 1878 and worked under Thomas Allen, exhibiting pieces at the Paris Exhibition. Although his work is relatively little known, he was an able decorator and worked for a number of other Staffordshire concerns such as William Brownfield of Cobridge and Wileman's Foley China Works of Fenton.

Portrait medallions (see Chapter 3), like jasper vases and teawares, continued to be made and included some new sitters. A convex green-ground jasper medallion (Fig. 106) depicts the great nineteenth-century botanist, Sir William Jackson Hooker (1785–1865). The same medallion is found incorporated into a fine memorial tablet of jasper ware and marble inside Kew Church on Kew Green.[40] The memorial was commissioned by the dead man's son, Joseph Dalton Hooker (1817–1911), who was also a botanist and took over from his father as Director of Kew Gardens. Joseph Hooker, who once owned the British Museum plate from the so-called 'Water Lily' service (see p. 128) was a keen Wedgwood collector, beginning in the 1860s, and was principally attracted by medallions and plaques. Through his friend Charles Darwin he became acquainted with the Wedgwoods, visiting Etruria where he explored the mould-chamber containing original moulds, and had several plaques reproduced by the firm. Hooker's Wedgwood collection numbering several hundred items was sold at Christie's in February 1917. The commissioning of his father's monument is recorded in correspondence preserved in the Wedgwood archives. The monument was designed by Hooker's cousin Reginald Palgrave and the medallion by Thomas Woolner, the pre-Raphaelite sculptor and poet. On the memorial the jasper ware portrait is in white on a blue ground and is surrounded by four green jasper slabs with groups of ferns; above is another slab containing a design in relief of wheat and grass and a crucifix. The small medallion in the British Museum may have been a trial piece, or may even have been made specially for friends of the dead man. There is a square example in blue jasper ware in the Royal Scottish Museum,[41] with its own satin-lined box stamped in gold with the name of the Manchester jewellers Olivant and Botsford.

In the later part of the nineteenth century one of the most widely used ceramic bodies was the lead-glazed earthenware known as 'majolica'. This highly coloured pottery was developed at Minton under its French-born Art Director Léon Arnoux, in time for the Great Exhibition of 1851. It was soon being made by many Staffordshire concerns and was imitated on the Continent. The majolica glazes could be fired up to 1,500°C, according to the colour, and were used on a once-fired earthenware body which had received a coating of opaque white glaze. The name 'majolica' derives from the 'maiolica' produced in Renaissance Italy, since the basis of this was also earthenware decorated in bright colours over an opaque white glaze, which in this case contained ashes of tin. However, despite the eclecticism of the mid-nineteenth century and its historicist tendency,

Figure 106 Convex green jasper dip medallion of Sir William Jackson Hooker (1785–1865), probably commissioned by his son Joseph Dalton Hooker as there is a similar one in a memorial tablet erected by the son in Kew Church, Surrey, in 1867. Impressed SIR W J HOOKER, WEDGWOOD. H. 2⅝ in (6.7 cm). Presented by A. W. Franks Esq.

most English majolica exhibits relatively little influence from fifteenth- and sixteenth-century Italian maiolica.

Majolica was not made in quantity at Wedgwood until the 1860s.[42] It is not the type of pottery which is generally associated with the Etruria factory, yet an extremely diverse and extensive range of pieces were put into production. Until lately these have not appealed to collectors and are not well represented in museums in Britain. A recent purchase of a majolica punch bowl ornamented with four heads of Punch and standing on four feet modelled as his dog, Toby (Fig. 107), is one of a small group of majolica pieces to enter the British Museum collections. Although its bright colours are characteristic of the material, it is an exceptional piece. It was probably part of a set, since there exist two beakers on a stand with the same unusual decoration.[43] The set is likely to have been made around 1878 on the evidence of 'ivory' tableware ornamented with printed and moulded Punch subjects, the design of which was registered at the Patent Office in 1878. A colour page from a contemporary publication showing the punch bowl was found not long ago on the Wedgwood Museum premises. It is probably an advertisement for majolicas from a trade journal but cannot yet be accurately dated.

Finally, a brief survey of a few products by the Wedgwood factory in the twentieth century should be made. A jardinière by the French designer Paul Follot (1877–1941) is a recent acquisition (Fig. 108). It is not widely known that at the beginning of the twentieth century several French designers were employed by Wedgwood and links established with the most fashionable retailing concerns in France. Paul Follot, who had designed for Julius Meier-Graefe's shop *La Maison Moderne* in Paris from 1901 and later became director of the

Figure 107 Majolica, or lead-glazed earthenware, punch-bowl ornamented with figures of Punch and his dog Toby. The bowl is dark blue, its interior lilac, the dogs brown, and Punch's hat yellow, impressed WEDGWOOD, probably *c.* 1878. Diam. 11¾ in (30 cm).

145

Figure 108 Creamware jardinère decorated by Bert Bentley with white slip under a clear lead glaze and ornamented with apples and leaves in high relief after a design called 'Pomona' by Paul Follot (1877–1941) in the Art Deco style, impressed WEDGWOOD, printed in black WEDGWOOD ETRURIA ENGLAND, 1921. H. to rim 8½ in (21.7 cm).

Atelier d'Art at the Paris department store *Le Bon Marché*,[44] was responsible for both Wedgwood tablewares and ornamental pieces. He signed a two-year agreement with the firm in March 1912. An extension of the period was interrupted by the outbreak of the First World War, but Follot recommenced work for the firm in 1919. His jardinière is a rare example of his highly individual style applied to ceramics. It is in the spirit of Art Deco, the movement which in France succeeded Art Nouveau, replacing its sinuosities with a formalism which was a reaction to the preceding era. The fruit design, which is called 'Pomona', can be seen in the Shapes Book kept at the Wedgwood factory. It was used not only for jardinières but also for compotiers, vases, flower trays and tureens.

Additional factory records show that the modeller Bert Bentley (active 1891–1936), who is often considered as one of the most skilful who ever worked for Wedgwood, spent considerable time in 1921 decorating a set of Pomona pieces, which were also made in basalt. Bentley was almost certainly chosen to work on interpreting Follot's designs because they were difficult to manufacture. The ornamentation is a *tour de force* of craftsmanship and it can be only on account of the large amounts of time spent on these pieces that so few appear to have been made. The lidded, rather bulbous piece described in Bert Bentley's price book as a 'glorified soup tureen' has '24 hrs' beside it, the jardinière, a less complicated item, '12 hrs'. The British Museum jardinière is a remarkable production since the French style remained in the main home-grown, and few examples of French design were interpreted outside their country of origin.

Better known are vases with matt glazes which remained in production for a considerable period (Pl. 16). Designed by the architect Keith Murray (1892–1981), they are amongst the most elegant and stylish pieces to emerge from the factory this century and show a remarkable awareness of contemporary design developments.

Murray joined the firm in 1933, was awarded the title Royal Designer in 1938,

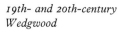

Figure 109 Pottery figure of a seated polar bear with a matt pale grey glaze, designed by John Skeaping PRA (1901–80), and first produced in 1927; printed in blue WEDGWOOD ETRURIA ENGLAND, MADE IN ENGLAND, impressed John Skeaping, *c.* 1935–9. H. 7⅛ in (18.2 cm).

and was joint architect, with C. S. White FRIBA, of the new factory opened at Barlaston in 1940. He was responsible for a large number of shapes, mainly for ornamental ware but also for some tableware such as sugar boxes, coffee pots and beakers. The glazes used on Murray's pieces, which were thrown and then turned on the lathe before firing, were often matt and then colours carefully chosen to co-ordinate with contemporary interiors. The uncluttered forms were in the spirit of the 1930s, and the classic proportions of the two Museum vases give them a lasting appeal. The designs are shown in the *Wedgwood Catalogue of Bodies, Glazes and Shapes*, which was presented by the Wedgwood firm to the Museum Department in 1941.

During the twentieth century the Wedgwood firm has not neglected the manufacture of figures. One range which has enjoyed fairly continuous popularity is the series of animal figures designed by John Skeaping PRA (1901–80) and put into production in 1927. Skeaping was at that time a most promising sculptor who had completed his studies abroad after winning the Prix de Rome in 1924. He was acclaimed by critics such as John Grierson, who drew attention to Skeaping's 'respect for form' and called him 'the chief exponent of the younger school'.[45] However, his reputation was eclipsed by Barbara Hepworth, to whom he was briefly married, and by Henry Moore. Skeaping's reputation now mainly rests on his animal drawings and sculptures, and particularly on his horse studies.

The British Museum has recently acquired a figure of a seated polar bear designed by Skeaping with a pleasing satin grey glaze (Fig. 109) which can be identified as one of the matt glazes. These were developed in 1933 and are mentioned in the introduction to the catalogue of the Grafton Galleries Exhibition held from 23 April to 12 May 1936 in London. In the *Wedgwood Catalogue of Bodies, Glazes and Shapes* the glaze is credited to the firm's research laboratory, and it is likely to have been developed by Norman Wilson, the factory's glaze chemist, who joined the firm as works manager in 1927 and has also worked in another capacity as a designer of tableware. The glaze enjoyed only a brief production life,[46] and the piece can be presumed to have been made between 1933 and 1940 since earthenware production moved to the Barlaston factory in 1940. The Skeaping animal figures were listed in the Grafton Galleries catalogue (p. 13), the price of the moonstone polar bear being given as 13s 6d. It was by no means the most expensive group since the 'Tiger and Buck' sold at £1 5s 6d.

Although Wedgwood productions of the nineteenth and twentieth centuries are still less well regarded than their eighteenth-century counterparts, they are becoming increasingly well known. It is now clear that these pieces too reveal the preoccupations of their age. They represent especially well the eclecticism of the Victorian era and, later, show how the firm responded to changes in aesthetic values ushered in with the advent of the 'modern style' in the early part of the twentieth century.

Appendix: Early copies of the Portland Vase

Compiled in association with Miss Ann Eatwell of the Victoria and Albert Museum.

ABBREVIATIONS

Meteyard, *Handbook*   E. Meteyard, *The Wedgwood Handbook*, London, 1875

Cook, *Old Wedgwood*   John Cook, 'Wedgwood's Copies of the Portland Vase', *Old Wedgwood*, Wellesley, Mass., 6, 1939

Numbered 'first edition' copies.

1 Washington, D.C., Smithsonian Institute, on anon. loan since 1972; Delhom Coll., 1961; Duff-Dunbar Coll., 1954–61; in the Holt Coll.; bt from Wedgwood by Apsley Pellatt, 1829.

2 Not at Barlaston, Staffs., Wedgwood Museum, as stated in *Josiah Wedgwood: 'the Arts and Sciences United'*, exh. cat., Science Museum, 1978, no. 170.

3 Dr Leonard Rakow, USA, bt Sotheby's, 22 Oct. 1974, lot 182; in Barker family since time of Richard Barker, friend of Thomas Bentley.

4 London, British Museum, gift of Mr and Mrs Isaac Falcke, 1909; exh. by Isaac Falcke, Crystal Palace, 1856 (*Art Journal, 1856*); from the coll. of Dr Lawrence, Ealing; 1909, 12–1, 88.

5 Untraced.

6 Said by B. Tattersall (*Wedgwood Review*, Dec. 1974, p. 12) to have been in the 'Berlin Museum' in the nineteenth century and to have been taken by Lord Macartney to Peking in 1792. Boston, USA, Museum of Fine Arts, numbered 6, 7, W; gift to Lloyd E. Hawes, 1958; sold by Miss E. Fisher, Sotheby's, 30 Oct. 1956, lot 96; probably belonged to Mr Rickman, 1875 (Meteyard, *Handbook*, p. 305) and reputed to have come from Apsley Pellatt; reg. 58.389.

7 Port Sunlight, Lady Lever Art Gallery, bt by Lord Leverhulme at Tweedmouth sale, 1905; bt by Lord Tweedmouth from Samuel Rogers's sale, 1856. Rogers (1763–1855) inherited money in 1793; reg 1204.

8 Manchester, Manchester Museum, beq. to University Museum by Jesse Haworth, 1937; Meteyard, *Handbook*, p. 305: 'Mr Phillips, silversmith and jeweller of Bond Street, has a copy numbered 8 in pencil on the lip.'

9 Boston, USA, Fogg Art Museum, in pencil on lip 9 and TREVOR; Winthrop Beq., 1943; bt by Winthrop from Rathbone (dealer), 1914; apparently from Sir Richard Tangye Coll.; sold by Mrs Winans, 1882; bt by Mrs Winans from Phillips, London, 1876, through 'a nephew by the name of Trevor'. His Excellency John Trevor subscribed to a copy he received on 22 Dec. 1797; he paid £27 11s on 12 Feb. 1799; reg. 1943. 1181.

10 Untraced.

11 Untraced.

12 Birmingham, Ala., USA, Museum of Art, acq. from Dwight and Lucille Beeson Coll., bt by Beesons 1965; had belonged to Sir Robin Darwin (loan to Victoria and Albert Museum, London, 1959–65); said to have belonged to Bernard Darwin, Charles Darwin, Dr R. W. Darwin, Erasmus Darwin to whom it was given by Josiah Wedgwood, 1789; reg. BMA 83.26.

13 Untraced.

14 Untraced.

15 Not in British Museum as stated by Meteyard, *Handbook*, p. 305.

16 Untraced.

17 Not Joseph Mayer's copy, Liverpool, County Museum (reg. M 2827 unnumbered) as stated in *Wedgwood Review*, Dec. 1974, p. 12.

18 Untraced.

19 Untraced.

20 Untraced.

21 Untraced.

22 Paul H. Lauer Coll., USA, sold from Oster Coll. Sotheby's, 30 Nov. 1971, lot 112; bt by Samuel B. Oster from a dealer, 1953; from coll. of Lt.-Gen. Alfred Codrington, GCVO, KCB, and probably in Codrington family from 1836; original owner Dowager Duchess of Beaufort (d. 1831), bt after 1799 when mentioned in Byerley's pocket book 'Copy not received up to 1799'.

23 Untraced.

24 Untraced.

25 Not at Barlaston, Staffs., Wedgwood Museum, as stated in *Josiah Wedgwood: 'the Arts and Sciences United'*, exh. cat., Science Museum, 1978, no. 169.

26 Private coll., USA. Formerly in possession of Dr Francis Vurpillat, Ind., USA, through his father Iva Vurpillat (from file, Victoria and Albert Museum).

27 Port Sunlight, Lady Lever Art Gallery, bt by Lord Leverhulme at Tweedmouth sale, 1905; beq. to Lord Tweedmouth by Lady Murray, widow of Sir John Murray, 1848; reg. 1206.

28 Sheffield, City Museum, anon. loan (Apr. 1983–Nov. 1983); from coll. of the late R. Ronald Copeland; bt from Robert Hoe sale, American Art

Assoc., Gilman Collamore, New York, 1929 (Ronald Copeland owned two copies of the vase c. 1937, but present whereabouts of second unknown).

29 Nottingham, Castle Museum, beq. by Felix Joseph, 1892; bt by Joseph from Sir William Tite's sale (through A. Wertheimer); bt by Tite at Purnell sale, Sotheby's, May 1872, through Jackson; said to have been bt by Purnell B. Purnell from a descendant of the Wedgwood family, 1830; reg. 92.472.

30 Chicago, USA, Art Institute; formerly Harry Manaster Coll. given by his daughter, 1979; from Col. G. I. Malcolm Coll.; Argyll, Scotland, through his great grandfather, John Malcolm; bt from an unknown Staffs. coll., c. 1860–90. reg. 1979.738.

Unnumbered 'first edition' copies

1 London, Victoria and Albert Museum, acq. 1956 through Tulk Beq.; bt by John Tulk at the sale of Charles Augustus Tulk, decd., Bullock, 3 Aug. 1849; Charles Tulk was a friend of John Flaxman jun. and is said to have bt the vase in 1829 on closure of Wedgwood's London showroom; reg. Circ. 732–1956.

2 London, Victoria and Albert Museum, transf. from Museum of Practical Geology, Jermyn Street, 1901; acq. between 1855 and 1866 (on evidence of catalogues), reputed to have come from Charles Darwin, whose father, Dr R. W. Darwin, bt it from Josiah Wedgwood in 1793; a letter in Wedgwood Archive to Josiah Wedgwood II states: 'I am infinitely obliged for your father's kind intention respecting the Portland Vase, but should think myself sufficiently gratified in being allowed to have it on the terms mentioned in my last.' reg. 2418–1901 (not numbered 28 as stated elsewhere).

3 London, Victoria and Albert Museum, Jones Coll., dark blue-black; beq. 1882 by Jones who owned it in 1875 (Meteyard, Handbook, p 303); reg. 854–1882.

4 Cambridge, Fitzwilliam Museum, on loan since 1963 from George Pember Darwin, direct descendant of Erasmus Darwin to whom it is said to have been given by Josiah Wedgwood I.

5 Liverpool, County Museum, beq. by Joseph Mayer (1803–86); in Mayer's possession 1875 (Meteyard, Handbook, p. 303); reg. M 2827 (base detached).

6 Barlaston, Staffs., Wedgwood Museum, supposedly numbered 2, acq. 1950; formerly belonged to Mr Eustace Calland, 31 Gilston Road, London, s.w.10 (Cook, Old Wedgwood, p. 63); bt by Thomas Hope of Amsterdam from the firm, 13 June 1793, for £31 10s, the case £2 10s; reg. unknown.

7 Barlaston, Staffs., Wedgwood Museum, supposedly numbered 25, 'a' in pencil on lip, said to be Josiah Wedgwood's own copy; reg. unknown.

8 Barlaston, Staffs., Wedgwood Museum, beq. by Ralph Vaughan Williams, probably in 1958 (from Leith Hill Place); recorded in Museum 1965. Vaughan Williams was a direct descendant of Josiah Wedgwood and Erasmus Darwin; reg. unknown.

9 Kingston upon Hull, City Museums and Art Galleries, supposed to have been destroyed by enemy action 1943; beq. by Mrs Peck of Scarborough; had belonged to M. C. Peck, printer and Freemason of Hull; in Museum 1929 (T. Sheppard, Hull Museum Treasures, 1929, pp. 3–4).

10 Edinburgh, Royal Scottish Museum, thought to be a 'first edition'; presented to University of Edinburgh 1815 by Josiah Wedgwood II (Cook, Old Wedgwood, p. 66); transf. to the Museum, presumably on its foundation in 1854; reg. U.C. 41.

11 Formerly at Leeds, Temple Newsam House, on loan from Trustees of the late W. H. Harding; scratches around lip, discoloration of reliefs in parts; apparently from Rathbone: said to have belonged to Lord Rodney, sold at Christie's, 10 October 1983, lot 123.

12 Private coll., USA, bt by Lawrence Pucci, Sotheby's, 1 July 1963, from Miss Denise Critchley Salmonson, a collateral of Duke of Portland; sold from Duke of Marlborough Coll., Christie's, 4 Aug. 1886, recorded in Blenheim Inventory, March 1884; an example delivered to Duke of Marlborough 1797.

13 Toledo, Ohio, USA; gift of Alfred B. Koch, 1923, thought to be a 'first edition', said to have belonged to R. and G. Tangye (Sir Richard Tangye, Old Wedgwood and Old Wedgwood Ware, Handbook to the Collection formed by Richard and George Tangye, London, 1885, no. 2844) and then to F. Rathbone; formerly in Bragg Coll.; reg. 23.3101.

14 Private coll., New York, sold Sotheby's, 27 May 1975, lot 177; belonged to Richard Pool King of Brislington, 1875 (Meteyard, Handbook, p. 303); said to have been presented to Thomas Poole of Nether Stowey by Josiah Wedgwood II, 1802.

15 Mr Keith Deutsher, Melbourne, Australia; acq. Feb. 1974 from D. Bernheim, New Jersey, USA, sold Christie's, 21 June, 1970, lot 303.

16 Private coll., England, blue-black jasper; by descent from Sir William Watson Cheyne of Shetland Islands; said to have been a gift to him from Lady Asquith c. 1910.

17 Merion, Pa., USA, Buten Museum of Ceramics; blistered; acq. 1954; reg. 6805 1250.

18 Merion, Pa., USA, Buten Museum of Ceramics; blistered; acq. 1954; reg. 6795 125a.

19 Mr Sanderson's Coll. exh. cat. Edinburgh, Museum of Science and Art, 1901, no. 115; detached reliefs in parts.

20 Private coll., New York, USA, badly blistered, and neck distorted.

Early blue Portland Vases

1 London, British Museum; presented by John Wedgwood, 1802; mid-blue jasper; reg. Pottery Cat. I 711.

2 Birmingham, Ala., USA, Dwight and Lucille Beeson Coll. presented in 1983; sold Christie's, 30 Nov. 1964, lot 57, and 13 June 1902, lot 474, Dr D. J. Propert Coll., Spranger Coll., reg. BMA 83.25.

3 Private coll., New York; 'wreathed effect' in blue jasper dip; red leather travelling case; sold Sotheby's, 20 Oct. 1981, lot 109, from Sneyd family; said to have been purchased from the firm by Dr John Sneyd of Belmont, Nr Leek, Staffs., on 4 Feb. 1801; he originally subscribed to the vase as in Thomas Byerley's notebook, 1789.

4 Merion, Pa., USA, Buten Museum of Ceramics; sky blue; said to have come from Tulk Coll. reg. 1032.

5 Mr Keith Deutsher, Melbourne, Australia, sold Sotheby's, 20 Nov. 1979, lot 57.

Notes

ABBREVIATIONS

Bindman, *John Flaxman, R.A.*	D. Bindman (ed.), *John Flaxman, R.A.*, exh. cat., Royal Academy of Arts, London, 26 October–9 December, 1979
ECC *Trans*	English Ceramic Circle *Transactions*
Finer and Savage, *Selected Letters*	A. Finer and G. Savage (eds), *The Selected Letters of Josiah Wedgwood*, London, 1965
Hobson, *Porcelain*	R. L. Hobson, *Catalogue of English Porcelain in the British Museum*, London, 1905
Hobson, *Pottery*	R. L. Hobson, *Catalogue of English Pottery in the British Museum*, London, 1903
Letters	*Letters of Josiah Wedgwood, 1762–1795* (introduction by B. Tattersall), 3 vols, pub. E. J. Morten, Manchester, 1973
Meteyard, *Life*	E. Meteyard, *The Life of Josiah Wedgwood*, London, 1866, vol. II
Prog. Wedg. Soc.	*Proceedings of the Wedgwood Society*

Introduction: Wedgwood's early years

1 Much information on early eighteenth-century Staffordshire has been drawn from Lorna Weatherill, *The Pottery Trade and North Staffordshire 1660–1760*, Manchester, 1971.

2 J. V. G. Mallet, 'John Baddeley of Shelton, Part I', *ECC Trans*, vol. 6, pt 2, 1966; pp. 124–66; 'Part II', ibid., vol. 6, pt 3, 1967, pp. 181–247.

Chapter 1 The 'useful' partnership

1 Finer and Savage, *Selected Letters*, pp. 34–8.

2 For agate and tortoise-shell wares see Hobson, *Pottery*.

3 Cyril Williams-Wood, *English Transfer–Printed Pottery and Porcelain*, London, 1981. See also Colin Wyman, 'The Early Techniques of Transfer-Printing', ECC *Trans*, vol. 10, pt 4, 1980, pp. 187–99.

4 The entire correspondence between Wedgwood and John Sadler and Guy Green is collected under the document reference Mosley 1431. Unless otherwise stated all letters quoted in the text bear this reference.

5 See Hobson, *Pottery*, cat. H 41. Illus. D. Towner, *Creamware*, London, 1978, pls 1A, 1B, p. 24.

6 Quoted Towner, op. cit., p. 44.

7 Quoted Finer and Savage, *Selected Letters*, p. 7.

8 Hobson, *Pottery*, cat. I 794.

9 This scene is the first plate entitled 'Bridge over the Ilissus – Temple of Pola in Istria'. I am most grateful to Mr Richard Gray of Manchester City Art Gallery for supplying this reference.

10 All patterns referred to occur in MS Mosley 1431, on loan to Keele University.

11 1909, 12–1, 456.

12 Bernard Rackham, *Catalogue of English Porcelain, Earthenware, Enamels and Glass collected by Charles Schreiber Esq., M.P. and the Lady Charlotte Elizabeth Schreiber . . .*, London, 1930, vol. II, cat. 401, pl. 57.

13 This jewel, uncatalogued and lacking any accession number, is on display in the Grand Lodge Library and Museum at the Freemasons' Hall, London. I am grateful to Mr J. Groves, Assistant Curator, for bringing it to my attention.

14 See Williams-Wood, op. cit., fig. 70, for an illustration of this design on a tea-caddy in private hands.

15 Cyril Cook, *Supplement to the Life and Work of Robert Hancock*, Knebworth, 1955, item 158; he quotes C. Gatty's catalogue of an exhibition held at the Liverpool Art Club, 1879, no. 1441.

Chapter 2 Wedgwood and Bentley and the 'ornamental' partnership

1 E.25–18120.

2 See Josiah C. Wedgwood MP, *A History of the Wedgwood Family*, London, 1909, pp. 173–5.

3 E.25–18123.

4 Mosley 1713.

5 Reproduced in facsimile in Mrs Robert D. Chellis, 'Wedgwood and Bentley Source Books', *7th Wed Wedgwood International Seminar*, Chicago, 1962, pp. 60–4.

6 T. Martyn and J. Lettice (trans.), *The Antiquities of Herculaneum*, London, 1773.

7 B. de Montfaucon, *L'Antiquité Expliquée et Représentée en Figures*, Paris, 1719–24.

8 J. V. G. Mallet, 'Wedgwood's Early Vases: The Collection at Saltram House, Devon', *Country Life*, 9 June 1966, pp. 1480–2.

9 Timothy Clifford, 'Some English Vases and their Sources, Part I,' *ECC Trans*, vol. 10, pt 3, 1978, pp. 159–73.

10 *Second Livre de Vases*, aux Galeries du Louvre chez Claudine Stella, 1667, referred to by Josiah Wedgwood as 'Stella's Vases', p. 26. I am grateful to Mrs Elizabeth Chellis for letting me examine Josiah Wedgwood and Thomas Bentley's own copy of this book now in her possession.

11 Dr G. C. Williamson, *The Imperial Russian Dinner Service*, London, 1909, frontispiece.

12 J. V. G. Mallet, 'Wedgwood and the Rococo', *Proc. Wedg. Soc.*, 9, 1975, pp. 56–7.

13 See Hobson, *Porcelain*, II 309, pl. XIX. There is

moulded leafage on the shoulder and foot, not found on Wedgwood's creamware ewer.

14 Letter of 11 April 1772, E.25–18365.
15 Another smaller Wedgwood ewer of the same shape but with marbled decoration of pale blue-grey, orange, pink and brown on a black basalt base is in the British Museum (1909, 12–1, 447).
16 Clifford, op. cit., pl. 82.
17 1909, 12–1, 443.
18 Illus. Captain M. H. Grant, *The Makers of Black Basaltes*, London, 1910, pls VI, fig. 2, and VII, fig. 2.
19 Pierre François Hugues, called Baron d'Hancarville, *Collection of Etruscan, Greek and Roman Antiquities in the Cabinet of the Hon.*^ble *W*^m *Hamilton*, vol. 1, Naples, 1766, pl. 54. See Charlotte Zeitlin, 'Wedgwood Copies of a Vase in the Hamilton Collection', *Proc. Wedg. Soc.*, 7, 1968, pp. 147–51, for illustrations of exact copies by Wedgwood of the Apulian *volute-krater*.
20 Finer and Savage, *Selected Letters*, pp. 206–7.
21 Grant, op. cit., ch. III, *passim*.
22 Hobson, *Pottery*, cat. G 40.
23 *Stonewares and Stone Chinas of Northern England to 1851*, exh. cat., City Museum and Art Gallery, Stoke-on-Trent, September–December 1982, p. 59.
24 Correspondence to the author from Mr David Barker, Department of Archaeology, Hanley Museum, Stoke-on-Trent. There are fragments of high-fired black ware from Whieldon's pottery at Fenton in both the British Museum and Victoria and Albert Museum collections, but they are not accurately datable.
25 These notebooks are the property of Josiah Wedgwood and Sons Ltd: some are kept at the Wedgwood Museum; others are loaned to Keele University Library, Staffordshire.
26 Hobson, *Pottery*, cat. I 341–559, intaglios in black basalt; cat. I 151–296 are jasper cameos and intaglios.
27 C. Gere, J. Rudoe, H. Tait, T. Wilson, *The Art of the Jeweller, A Catalogue of the Hull Grundy Gift to the British Museum*, London, 1984, cat. 863.
28 A lioness is shown in a similar pose on a classical gem illustrated by G. Lippold, *Gemmen und Kameen des Altertums und der Neuzeit*, Stuttgart, n.d. (?1922), Tafel LXXXVI, 7.
29 O. M. Dalton, *Catalogue of the Engraved Gems of the Post-Classical Periods*, London, 1915, various items.
30 John Goldsmith Phillips, 'Gugliemo della Porta – His Ovid Plaquettes', *Bulletin of the Metropolitan Museum of Art*, June 1939, pp. 148–51.
31 Hugh Tait, 'The Wedgwood Collection in the British Museum, Part II: Basalt and Jasper Wares', *Proc. Wedg. Soc.*, 5, 1963, pl. 8, fig. 16. It is marked WEDGWOOD, is considerably warped and is not 'bronzed'.
32 See Bindman, *John Flaxman, R.A*
33 I am grateful to Miss Gaye Blake Roberts of the Wedgwood Museum for allowing me to read her unpublished lecture to the Wedgwood Society in 1983 on sculptors working with Flaxman in Rome entitled 'New thoughts on an old theme: 18th century Wedgwood'. There are several plaques in the British Museum collection with designs by Pacetti: Priam kneeling before Achilles begging the body of his son Hector (1909, 12–1, 206), Endymion on Mount Latmos (1909, 12–1, 208) and the 'Tri-form Diana'

(1909, 12–1, 207), all on rectangular green jasper dip plaques; on a rectangular dark blue jasper dip plaque is Aesculapius and Hygeia (1909, 12–1, 191).
34 Illus. M. Thirion, *Les Adam et les Clodion*, Paris, 1885, p. 355. Monsieur Ojalvo, of the Musée des Beaux Arts, has kindly confirmed that there is a 'vase en biscuit' of this form measuring 37 cm in height by Clodion in the collections. It is not stated whether this piece is signed. Clodion's career also included work for the Niderviller porcelain factory.
35 F. J. B. Watson, *Wallace Collection : Catalogue of Furniture*, London, 1956, F 348–9.
36 *Letters*, vol. II, pp. 39–40.
37 John Rylands Library, Manchester, English MS 1110.
38 F. Haskell and N. Penny, *Taste and the Antique*, New Haven and London, 1981, fig. 138, no. 61.
39 See Meteyard, *Life*, pp. 78–81, where a section of the patent is reproduced.
40 A. de Ridder, *Bronzes Antiques du Louvre*, Paris, 1915, vol. 2, no. 2955.
41 I am grateful to the Hon. Mrs Jane Roberts, Curator of the Print Room, Windsor Castle, for providing information about this drawing. An account of the provenance of the dal Pozzo drawings is given in A. Blunt, 'The History of the Royal Collection of Drawings', in Edmund Schilling, *The German Drawings in the Collection of her Majesty the Queen at Windsor Castle*, London and New York, 1971, pp. 8–9.
42 Department of Greek and Roman Antiquities, 1824, 4–89, 87. I am grateful to members of this Department for their assistance in tracing the history of the classical bronze.
43 Grant, op. cit., pl. LVII, fig. 2.
44 F. Rathbone, *Old Wedgwood*, London, 1898, pl. LXII.
45 'Continuation of a Paper on the Production of Light and Heat', paper read by Thomas Wedgwood before the Royal Society, 10 May 1792, published in *Philosophical Transactions*, vol. 82, 1792, II, pp. 270–82. An offprint inscribed by Thomas to his brother John is MS 40–28420 on loan to Keele University from Josiah Wedgwood and Co. Ltd.
46 Documents numbered E.95–17650 refer to silver cylinders, ordered from Mr Burley of Birmingham, rather than earthenware ones.
46a A. T. Green, 'The Contributions of Josiah Wedgwood to the Technical Side of the Pottery Industry', *Transactions of the Ceramic Society*, XXIX, 5, May 1930, p. 13.
47 *Letters*, vol. II, p. 42.
48 Finer and Savage, *Selected Letters*, p. 311.
49 A pair of candlesticks with black reliefs including a lotus motif impressed WEDGWOOD and A are 1909, 12–1, 109.
50 *Letters*, vol. II, p. 3.
51 E.25–18432.
52 E.25–18509.
53 A letter from Wedgwood to Bentley of 24 August 1770, E.25–18320, mentions various books he is going to consult and others with which he has been presented. A companion medallion to Flora showing Omphale or Iole is also related to a classical gem (1909, 12–1, 225).
54 A gem of this subject which is not unlike the Wedgwood plaque is illustrated in Lippold, op. cit., Tafel LXXVI, no. 10. The marble which once belonged to Hamilton is not in the British Museum.

55 P. de Stosch, *Pierres Antiques Gravées*, Amsterdam, 1724, pl. LXX.

56 See n. 5 above.

57 1909, 12–1, 219.

58 1915, 12–16, 20.

59 For a discussion of the work and identity of Moderno, see J. Pope-Hennessy, *Renaissance Bronzes from the Samuel H. Kress Collection*, London, 1965, pp. 42–56.

60 D. Buten, *18th Century Wedgwood*, New York, 1980, pl. XIII.

61 Information kindly supplied by Mrs Lynn Miller, Wedgwood Museum.

62 Finer and Savage, *Selected Letters*, p. 270.

63 Illus. in C. Macht, *Classical Wedgwood Designs*, New York, 1957, pp. 67–8.

64 Lynn Miller, 'The Oven Books: Oddities and Incidentals', *Proc.Wedg.Soc.*, 11, 1982, p. 168.

65 Macht, op. cit., pp. 86–93.

66 Buten, op. cit., pl. 172, p. 165.

67 *Lord Leverhulme*, exh. cat., Royal Academy of Arts, London, 12 April–25 May 1980, p. 132.

68 ibid.

69 Bindman, *John Flaxman, R.A.*, pp. 60–1.

70 A. C. P. Tubière de Grimoard, de Pestels, de Levy, Comte de Caylus, *Receuil d'Antiquités Egyptiennes, Etrusques, Grecques et Romaines,* vol. III, Paris, 1759, pl. XL, II.

71 Buten, op. cit., fig. 157; there are five examples in the collection of Her Majesty the Queen. I am grateful to Mr Geoffrey de Bellaigue, CVO, Surveyor of the Queen's Works of Art, and Mrs Julia Harland for their help in examining these pieces.

72 Pouget Fils, *Traité des Pierres Précieuses et de la manière de les employer en Parure*, Paris, 1762, p. 56.

73 De Montfaucon, op. cit., vol. III, pt 2, pl. 173.

74 See n. 5 above.

75 Haskell and Penny, op. cit., no. 29, pp. 195–6.

76 E.25–18847.

77 A drawing of 'three children' is reproduced in Mrs Leonard S. Rakow, 'The Feminine Touch in Wedgwood', *12th Wedgwood International Seminar,* 1967, fig. 161, but the whereabouts of the drawing has not been given. It is probably the one shown as a coloured photogravure frontispiece to Mrs Steuart Erskine, *Lady Diana Beauclerk*, London, 1903, at that time in the collection of Col. Lascelles, Woolbeding.

78 I am grateful to Mr Geoffrey de Bellaigue, CVO, Surveyor of the Queen's Works of Art, for assisting my research into Wedgwood in the Royal Collection.

79 Hobson, *Pottery*, cat. I 748.

80 Harry Barnard, *Chats on Wedgwood Ware*, London, 1924, fig. 7, opp. p. 236.

81 Joan Evans, *A History of The Society of Antiquaries*, London, 1956.

82 1909, 12–1, 261.

83 This catalogue is kept in the Department of Medieval and Later Antiquities, British Museum.

84 Some of these are also illustrated in the catalogue of 'Goods in the Catacombs'.

Chapter 3 Wedgwood and portraits

1 E.25–18722.

2 Hobson, *Pottery*, cat. I 1–110 incl. Some portraits have now been re-identified.

3 A remarkable portrait plaque of the Empress Maria Theresa of Austria, *c.* 1745, is illustrated in L. Ginori Lisci, *La porcellana di Doccia*, Milan, 1963, pl. 17; see also tav. XXXVIII for a group dated 1756 representing a temple to the glory of Tuscany decorated with portraits in white on a blue ground.

4 Hugh Tait in 'Wedgwood, Flaxman and an English Eighteenth-Century Portrait Carver, Silvanus Bevan', *Proc. Wedg. Soc.*, 3, 1959, pp. 126–32, shows how an ivory carving of Dr Richard Mead was the basis of a jasper portrait (Pottery Cat. I 100) modelled by John Flaxman jun.

5 Department of Coins and Medals, M 6569. Illus. in L. Brown, *A Catalogue of British Historical Medals 1760–1960*, vol. I, 1980, no. 94, p. 1765.

6 *Trésor de Numismatique: Médailles Françaises*, pt II, pl. XXX.5; there is no example in the British Museum.

7 Department of Coins and Medals, George III English Medals, no. 47.

8 Finer and Savage, *Selected Letters*, pp. 34–8.

9 See Hobson, *Pottery*, for jasper medallions of the monarchs.

10 L.1–112.

11 E.25–18521.

12 1909, 12–1, 264.

13 Bindman, *John Flaxman, R.A.*, p. 69.

14 T. Hodgkinson, 'John Lochée, Portrait Sculptor', *Victoria and Albert Museum Yearbook*, 1, 1959, pp. 152–60.

15 Meteyard, *Life*, p. 507.

16 See Hodgkinson, op. cit., figs 2 (Prince of Wales), 3 (Adolphus Frederick, Duke of Cambridge – wrongly captioned), 4 (Prince Edward, Duke of Kent), 5 (Frederick Augustus, Duke of York).

17 ibid., fig. 4.

18 ibid., p. 152, and n. 5.

19 H. Barnard, 'The Etruria Museum', *Connoisseur*, May 1930, pp. 295–9.

20 1909, 12–1, 153.

21 Pottery Cat. I 54.

22 Correspondence between Mountstephen and Thomas Byerley on loan to Keele University, MS L 13–19 incl.

23 This bust was on loan anonymously to the National Portrait Gallery in 1973; reproduced in Robin Reilly, *Wedgwood Portrait Medallions*, exh. cat., National Portrait Gallery, London, 1973, cat. 23a.

24 See n. 22.

25 Pottery Cat. I 61, impressed 'Wedgwood & Bentley'.

26 The jasper version is reversed from the medal, Department of Coins and Medals, M 4837.

27 R. Reilly and G. Savage, *Wedgwood, the Portrait Medallions*, London, 1973, p. 365.

28 O. M. Dalton, *Catalogue of the Finger Rings . . . bequeathed by Sir Augustus Wollaston Franks, K.C.B.*, London, 1912, no. 1392, pl. XX.

29 Reilly and Savage, op. cit., pp. 182–3.

30 Pottery Cat. I 68, biscuit earthenware; 1909, 12–1, 127, black basalt.

31 Pottery Cat. I 60.

32 Cambridge University Library, MS Add. 6294.

33 Wedgwood Papers on loan to Keele University, Microfilm V, 127.

34 Timothy Clifford, 'Wedgwood at the National Portrait Gallery' (review of an exhibition of portrait medallions), *Burlington Magazine*, CXV, December

1973, pp. 832–5.

35 E.26–18887.

36 Reilly and Savage, op. cit., p. 259.

37 Reilly and Savage, op. cit., pp. 145–8. Examples in the British Museum collections of the earlier portraits are Pottery Cat. I 75; I 76; 1909, 12–1, 150, 1909, 12–1, 151 dates from 1777.

38 Pottery Cat. I 77.

39 E. V. Lucas, *David Williams, Founder of the Royal Literary Club*, London, 1920, pp. 8–9.

40 *Trésor de Numismatique*, vol. 9, Paris, 1836, pl. X, no. 5; Department of Coins and Medals, 1947-6-7-548, a button.

41 *The Man at Hyde Park Corner. Sculpture by John Cheere 1709–1787*, exh. cat., Temple Newsam, Leeds, 15 May–15 June 1974; Marble Hill House, Twickenham, 19 July–8 September 1974.

42 M. Bergmann, *Marc Aurel*, Frankfurt am Main, 1978, p. 22 and fig. 26.

43 Meteyard, *Life*, p. 325.

44 Information on this marble (inv. no. 16980) kindly supplied by Madame Coullery, Curator at the Musée d'Art et d'Histoire, Geneva.

45 It has not been scientifically examined, and no recent conservation work has been carried out.

Chapter 4 Painting on eighteenth-century Wedgwood

1 27 November 1775, E.25–18626.

2 Meteyard, *Life*, pp. 80–1. A. T. Green in 'The Contributions of Josiah Wedgwood to the Technical Side of the Pottery Industry, *Transactions of the Ceramic Society*, XXIX, 5, May 1930, quotes Bentley's 'Commonplace Book' under the date August 1773 to show that tin or clay, or 'vitrescent stones and tin' were used to prevent vitrification of the colours. Four recipes for encaustic colours are given.

3 See letter of 19 November 1769 quoted in D. Towner, *Creamware*, London, 1978, p. 52.

4 See D. Towner, *Creamware*, London, 1978, p. 58.

5 E.25–18189.

6 E.25–18255.

7 U. des Fontaines, 'Wedgwood's London Showrooms', *Proc. Wedg. Soc.*, 8, 1970, pp. 199–200.

8 R. Reilly, *The Collector's Wedgwood*, New York, 1980, fig. 142. The inscription is wrongly recorded and the correct date is 1774.

9 A. C. P. Tubière de Grimoard, de Pestels, de Levy, Comte de Caylus, *Receuil d'Antiquités Egyptiennes, Etrusques, Grecques et Romaines*, vol. II, Paris, 1756, pl. XLIII, 1.

10 See n. 5, Ch. 2.

11 Caylus, op. cit., pp. 124–6.

12 Pierre François Hugues, called Baron d'Hancarville, *Collection of Etruscan, Greek and Roman Antiquities in the Cabinet of the Hon.*ble *W.*m *Hamilton*, vol. II, Naples, 1767, pl. 45.

13 Letter from Wedgwood to Bentley, 20 September 1769, E.25–18258.

14 A. F. Gori, *Gemmae Antiquae ex Thesauro Mediceo . . .*, Florence, 1731, vol. I, pl. LXXIX, IV and V.

15 ibid., pl. LXXIV, V.

16 See d'Hancarville, op. cit., vol. I, 1785 edn, pl. 10.

17 Pietro Santi Bartoli, *Raccolta di Camei e Gemme Antiche*, Rome, 1727. The plate is unnumbered but is sixty-sixth in the sequence.

18 P. de Stosch, *Pierres Antiques Gravées*, Amsterdam, 1724, pl. XVI.

19 I am grateful to Mr Nicholas Turner for clarifying the symbolism of this scene.

20 The original is unknown; the engraving occurs on an invitation card held in the Department of Prints and Drawings (1871, 12–9, 5670), inscribed 'G R Cipriani inv: F. Bartolozzi sculp.'

21 A plaque decorated in orange and grey is illustrated in D. Buten, *18th Century Wedgwood*, New York, 1980, pl. XI.

22 Lady Victoria Manners and Dr G. C. Williamson, *Angelica Kauffmann, R.A.*, London, 1924, p. 143. A memorandum drawn up by the artist mentions under Rome, Jan. 1783 'Cleopatra lying at the feet of Augustus begging for mercy' painted on a circular copper plaque.

23 Hugh Tait, 'The Wedgwood Collection in the British Museum, Part I: Creamware and Redware', *Proc. Wedg. Soc.*, 4, 1961, p. 198.

24 Aubrey J. Toppin, 'William Hopkins Craft, Enamel Painter (1730?–1810)'; ECC *Trans*, vol. 4, pt 4, pp. 14–18, pl. 15.

25 Information kindly supplied by Mr Ian Jenkins, Department of Greek and Roman Antiquities.

26 Leslie Campbell Hatfield, 'A Set of English Silver Condiment Vases from Kedleston Hall', *Bulletin of the Museum of Fine Arts, Boston*, 79, 1981, pp. 4–19.

27 d'Hancarville, op. cit., vol. II, 1767, pl. 38.

28 Cecil H. Smith, *Catalogue of the Greek and Etruscan Vases in the British Museum*, vol. III, London, 1896, cat. E. 499.

29 D'Hancarville, op. cit., vol. II, pl. 41.

30 ibid., pl. 71 and vol. I, pl. 26 both bear similarities to the Wedgwood painted figure which seems to have been adapted rather than directly copied in this instance.

31 1909, 12–1, 474.

32 D'Hancarville, op. cit., vol. I, 1766, pl. 130.

33 Francis Grose, *The Antiquities of England and Wales*, London, 1773–87.

34 See Larissa Dukelskaya (comp.), *The Hermitage, English Art Sixteenth to Nineteenth Century*, Leningrad, 1979, nos 279–87 for selected examples.

35 Hugh Tait, 'Plate "190" in the Imperial Russian Service is reidentified', *Connoisseur*, July 1969, pp. 208–9.

36 Horace Walpole, *Observations on Modern Gardening*, London, 3rd edn 1771, pp. 184–93.

37 Department of Prints and Drawings, British Museum, English School, Woollett, vol. II, p. 28, first state (1866-12-8-99). The second state, ibid., p. 27 (1840-8-8-162) was 'for Robert Sayer' and others.

38 I am extremely grateful to Mr Michael Raeburn for supplying information on the sources and on the service in Leningrad which he has examined closely.

39 Dr G. C. Williamson, *The Imperial Russian Dinner Service*, London, 1909. A new study of the service is currently in preparation edited by Michael Raeburn.

40 Finer and Savage, *Selected Letters*, pp. 160–1.

41 Williamson, op. cit., pp. 35–6.

42 Quoted in James Harris, First Earl of Malmesbury, *Diaries and Correspondence*, London, 1844, vol. i, p. 231.

43 Four illustrated in monochrome by R. Tames, *Josiah Wedgwood*, Aylesbury, 1972, p. 27. Cup and saucer from Liverpool Museum, R. Reilly and G. Savage, *The Dictionary of Wedgwood*, Woodbridge, 1980, p. 159.

Chapter 5 The Pegasus Vase

1 I am grateful to members of the Department of Greek and Roman Antiquities, and in particular Mr Ian Jenkins, for help in identifying the classical elements.
2 Document in the possession of Mrs Robert D. Chellis, Boston, Mass. Quoted by V. J. Scheidemantel, 'The "Apotheosis of Homer": A Wedgwood & Bentley Plaque', in *Festschrift Ulrich Middeldorf*, A. Kosegarten and P. Tigler (eds), Berlin, 1968, see p. 520.
3 This document is now missing. Quoted by W. Mankowitz, *The Portland Vase and the Wedgwood Copies*, London, 1952, pp. 29–30.
4 Cecil H. Smith, *Catalogue of the Greek and Etruscan Vases in the British Museum*, vol. III, London, 1896, cat. E. 460, p. 282. The name of the shape has been amended by the Department of Greek and Roman Antiquities since the publication of the catalogue.
5 F. Haskell and N. Penny, *Taste and the Antique*, New Haven and London, 1981, no. 63, pp. 269–71.
6 B. de Montfaucon, *L'Antiquité Expliquée et Représentée en Figures*, Paris, 1719–24. There is a possible model in vol. III, pt I, pl. 121.
7 I am grateful to Mrs Lynn Miller of the Wedgwood Museum for this information. The 'Oven Book' is numbered 53–30016.
8 Illus. in colour by G. Wills, *Wedgwood*, London, 1980, fig. 43, p. 67.
9 This substance has not been scientifically analysed.
10 Illus. in colour on dust-jacket of W. Mankowitz, *Wedgwood*, London, 1953.
11 The other side is shown in E. Meteyard, *Choice Examples of Wedgwood's Art*, London, 1879, pl. XXIV.
12 Sales reference book and factory records of shapes kept at the Wedgwood Museum.
13 *Manual for the Department of Natural History and Antiquities*, n.d., paper watermarked 1805, p. 10. Kept in the central archives of the British Museum.
14 *A Guide to the English Pottery and Porcelain in the Department of British and Medieval Antiquities*, London, 1904, p. 69.

Chapter 6 The Portland Vase

1 D. E. L. Haynes, *The Portland Vase*, London, 2nd rev. edn, 1975.
2 Donald B. Harden 'New Light on the History and Technique of the Portland and Auldjo Cameo Vessels', *Journal of Glass Studies*, 25, 1983, pp. 45–54; Mavis Bimson and Ian C. Freestone, 'An Analytical Study of the Relationship Between the Portland Vase and Other Roman Cameo Glasses', ibid., pp. 55–64.
3 I am grateful to several members of the Department of Greek and Roman Antiquities, and especially Dr V. Tatton-Brown, for assistance in writing this chapter. The dating of the classical vase has been arrived at in the context of known classical cameo glass vessels.
4 Bernard Ashmole, 'A New Interpretation of the Portland Vase', *Journal of Hellenic Studies*, LXXXVII, 1967, pp. 1–17.
5 J. G. F. Hind, 'Greek and Roman epic scenes on the Portland Vase', *Journal of Hellenic Studies*, XCIX, 1979, pp. 20–5.
6 C. Vermeule, 'The Portland Vase before 1650, the Evidence of Certain dal Pozzo-Albani drawings at Windsor Castle and the British Museum', *3rd Annual Wedgwood Seminar*, 1958, pp. 59–70.
7 Pietro Santi Bartoli, *Gli Antichi Sepolchri*, Rome, 1697, pls 84–6.
8 Harden, op. cit., p. 45.
9 Vermeule, op. cit., *passim*.
10 G. Wills, 'Sir William Hamilton and the Portland Vase', *Apollo*, CX, September 1979, pp. 195–201, see p. 195.
11 Harden, op. cit., p. 50.
12 Dr and Mrs Leonard Rakow, 'New Facts on the Portland Vase and the Wedgwood Portlands', *16th Wedgwood International Seminar*, 1971, p. 214 and n. 1.
13 Unregistered. Illus. in Haynes, op. cit., pls X, XI.
14 Wills, op. cit., *passim*.
15 Wills, op. cit., p. 198.
16 Ibid., p. 195.
17 Horace Walpole, *Letters addressed to the Countess of Ossory*, London, 1848, vol. II, p. 235.
18 Wills, ibid., pp. 199–200.
19 Wills, ibid., p. 201.
20 E.33–24859.
21 See Ch. 2, n. 33.
22 See Ch. 2, n. 33.
23 See Ch. 2, n. 33.
24 MS L.1–155 on loan to Keele University.
25 See Ch. 2, n. 33.
25a See Ch. 5, n. 3.
26 Quoted Meteyard, *Life*, p. 581.
27 Geoffrey Keynes, *Blake Studies*, Oxford, 2nd edn 1971, pp. 59–65, quoted p. 60.
28 ibid.
29 I am grateful to Miss Ann Eatwell of the Victoria and Albert Museum for communicating this report to me.
30 E.82–14607.
31 *Letters*, vol. III, pp. 139–2.
32 Johanna W. A. Naber, *Correspondentie van de Stadhouderlijkefamilie 1775–1795*, s'Gravenhage, 1931, vol. I, p. 59.
33 E.33–24860.
34 E.32–5363, 5364.
35 Sotheby's, 20 October 1981, lot 109.
36 Apsley Pellatt (1791–1863) introduced and patented a process for cameo incrustation, enclosing white porcellaneous cameos and medallions in cut crystal glass. He owned the Whitefriars glass factory and was also a distinguished writer on glass topics.
37 On a miniature black jasper dip example (1909, 12–1, 87), $4\frac{1}{8}$ in (10.5 cm) in height, impressed WEDGWOOD, the male figure leaving the shrine is draped.
38 W. Chaffers, *Ceramic Art of Great Britain*, London, 1878, vol. 2, p. 254.

Chapter 7 Nineteenth- and twentieth-century
Wedgwood

1 U. des Fontaines, 'Portland House, Wedgwood's London Showrooms (1774–95)', *Proc. Wedg. Soc.*, 11, 1982, pp. 136–48. See also *idem*, 'Wedgwood's London Showrooms', op. cit., 8, 1970, pp. 193–212.

2 Illus. G. Wills, *Wedgwood*, 1980, p. 92.

3 See C. Jagger, *Royal Clocks*, London, 1983, no. 181, illus.

4 Sotheby's, French Furniture, 8 July 1983, lot 122.

5 Hugh Tait, 'The Wedgwood Collection in the British Museum, Part II: Basalt and Jasper Wares', *Proc. Wedg. Soc.*, 5, 1963, p. 37.

6 A. Kelly, 'Vulliamys, Wedgwoods and Georgian Clocks', *Proc. Wedg. Soc.*, 7, 1968, pp. 152–62, and *idem*, 'A Clockmaker's Taste for Ceramics', *Country Life*, 15 June 1967, pp. 1526–8.

7 B. and H. Wedgwood, *The Wedgwood Circle 1730–1897*, London, 1980. B. Wedgwood, 'John Wedgwood, 1766–1844' in *Wedgwood: Its Competitors and Imitators 1800–1830 (22nd Wedgwood International Seminar)*, vol. 22, 1977, pp. 251–65.

8 Alexandre Brongniart (1770–1847), author of a key work on the technique of ceramics, *Traité des arts céramiques*, pub. 1844, was director of the Sèvres porcelain factory between 1800 and 1847.

9 U. des Fontaines, 'The Darwin Service and the First Printed Floral Patterns at Etruria', *Proc. Wedg. Soc.*, 6, 1966, pp. 69–90.

10 ibid., p. 83–5.

11 1970, 1–4, 56; Diam. $7\frac{1}{4}$ in (18.4 cm).

12 I am grateful to Mrs Jennifer Woods of the Royal Botanic Garden, Edinburgh, for her assistance in identifying these plants.

13 U. des Fontaines, *Wedgwood Fairyland Lustre*, London and New York, 1975, pp. 9–15.

14 I am grateful to Mrs Solene Morris of the Department of Zoology, British Museum, Natural History, for help in identifying the shell forms.

15 Illus. in *Wedgwood: Its Competitors and Imitators 1800–1830 (22nd Wedgwood International Seminar)*, vol. 22, 1977, pl. X.

16 Mrs Sharon Gater, 'Enduring designs from "the wonderful works of nature"', *Wedgwood Review*, winter 1982, pp. 8–9.

17 U. des Fontaines, op. cit., pp. 14–15.

18 1909, 12–1, 477.

19 See P. Halfpenny (ed.), *Spode–Copeland 1733–1983*, exh. cat., City Museum and Art Gallery, Stoke-on-Trent, 1983.

20 J. K. des Fontaines FRSA, 'Wedgwood Bone China of the first Period', *Proc. Wedg. Soc.*, 10, 1979, pp. 87–103.

21 ibid.; see also U. des Fontaines FRSA, 'Early Printed Patterns at Etruria', op. cit., 9, 1975, pp. 1–21.

22 I am grateful to Mrs Jennifer Woods of the Royal Botanic Garden, Edinburgh, for this information.

23 G. Wills, 'Pots for Painting', *Proc. Wedg. Soc.*, 3, 1959, pp. 152–4.

24 Some are illustrated in *Wedgwood: Its Competitors and Imitators 1800–1830 (22nd Wedgwood International Seminar)*, vol, 22, 1977, pl. I.

25 W. D. John and T. Simcox, *Early Wedgwood Lustre Wares*, Newport, 1963.

26 U. des Fontaines, *Wedgwood Fairyland Lustre*, London and New York, 1975, p. 10.

27 See n. 24.

28 1909, 12–1, 475.

29 1909, 12–1, 462.

30 1909, 12–1, 465; 1909, 12–1, 446.

31 Wedgwood Papers on loan to Keele University, MS Mosley 1100.

32 Maureen Batkin, *Wedgwood Ceramics 1846–1959*, London, 1982, p. 28.

33 Hugh Tait, 'The Wedgwood Collection in the British Museum, Part I: Redware and Creamware', *Proc. Wedg. Soc.*, 4, 1961, p. 200.

34 Batkin, op. cit., pp. 17–20.

35 There is an example in black basalt illus. in H. Buten, *Wedgwood Rarities*, Merion (Pa.), 1969, p. 249.

36 Stated in a letter kept on file in the Department of Medieval and Later Antiquities, British Museum, from John Cook, apparently on internal evidence, to Mrs Jean Gorely dated 12 March 1935.

37 A clipping in the 'Wedgwood Scrapbook' compiled by Isaac Falcke kept in the Department of Medieval and Later Antiquities, British Museum, is marked 'Times May 14 1877', but this date is incorrect and the item has not so far been traced at Colindale Newspaper Library.

38 Another clipping in the Falcke Scrapbook is erroneously captioned 'Evening Standard December 24 1883'.

39 Reginald Haggar, 'Thomas Allen', *Proc. Wedg. Soc.*, 6, 1966, pp. 61–8; *idem*, 'Thomas Allen – a Further Note', op. cit., 7, 1968, pp. 186–9; Dean Rockwell, 'The Artistry of Thomas Allen', Wedgwood International Seminar, forthcoming.

40 J. B. Smith, 'Two Memorials in Jasper Ware', *Proc. Wedg. Soc.*, 3, 1959, pp. 141–8; see also LEH (Lloyd E. Hawes), 'Joseph Dalton Hooker MD (1817–1911), Enthusiastic Wedgwood Scholar', *The American Wedgwoodian*, December 1965, pp. 36–7.

41 Reg. no. 1968 838A.

42 Batkin, op. cit., p. 31.

43 Reg. no. 3389. The design registration mark impressed on the tray is illegible.

44 Jessica Rutherford, 'Paul Follot', *Connoisseur*, June 1980, pp. 86–91; *idem, Art Nouveau, Art Deco and The Thirties: The Furniture Collections at Brighton Museum*, 1983, p. 33; Maureen Batkin, 'Wedgwood Ware designed by Paul Follot', *The Decorative Arts Society Journal*, 7, 1983, pp. 26–33. I am grateful to Miss J. Rutherford for drawing my attention to these articles.

45 John Grierson, 'The New Generation in Sculpture', *Apollo*, XII, July–December 1930, pp. 347–51.

46 I am grateful to Mrs Sharon Gater of the Wedgwood Museum for this information.

Further reading

Barnard, Harry, *Chats on Wedgwood Ware*, London 1924

Finer, Ann, and Savage, George (eds), *The Selected Letters of Josiah Wedgwood*, London, 1965

Honey, W. B., *Wedgwood Ware*, London, 1948

Kelly, Alison, *Decorative Wedgwood in Architecture and Furniture*, London, 1965
The Story of Wedgwood, London, 1962

Meteyard, Eliza, *Life of Josiah Wedgwood*, 2 vols, London, 1865–6 (facsimile edn 1980)

Reilly, Robin, *Wedgwood Portrait Medallions*, exh. cat. National Portrait Gallery, London, 1973

Reilly, Robin, and Savage, George, *Wedgwood Portrait Medallions*, London, 1973

Tames, Richard, *Josiah Wedgwood*, Aylesbury, 1972 (especially written for young people)

Letters of Josiah Wedgwood, 1762–1795 (introduction by B. Tattersall), 3 vols, pub. E. J. Morten, Manchester, 1973

Josiah Wedgwood: 'the Arts and Sciences United', exh. cat., Science Museum, pub. Josiah Wedgwood and Sons Ltd, Barlaston, Staffordshire, 1978

Wedgwood, Small Picture Book no. 45, Victoria and Albert Museum, HMSO 1958

Index

Page numbers in italics refer to illustrations.